CONTENTS

PART ONE

LOOKING AFTER HOUSEPLANTS

PART TWO

PLANT DIRECTORY

KNOW THE BASICS

Each year, the popularity of houseplants increases and few people can resist having some flowering or foliage plants to transform their house into a home. Apart from creating colour and vibrancy, houseplants have a therapeutic quality: they are alive and need regular, careful attention, generating rapport with people throughout the year.

Given the fast pace of life today, and the pressure it creates in our lives, the restful atmosphere that can be engendered by houseplants is essential. The range of houseplants is wide, including flowering and foliage types, as well as indoor ferns, bromeliads, cacti and other succulents, palms and cycads, bulbs and insectivorous plants. All have different needs and whether your home is a bungalow or a high-rise flat there are plants that will thrive in it. Some are native to tropical and subtropical regions, while others are hardy enough to grow outdoors in temperate zones but can also be grown indoors when young and in a pot.

In the directory of houseplants in Part Two (*see* pages 38–154), you will find detailed information about each plant's needs, from warmth and light throughout the year, to watering and feeding, as well as how to increase plants.

Growing plants indoors is an all-embracing hobby. While some plants happily thrive on windowsills, others develop into large, eye-catching features that live for so long they become as much part of a home as a dog or cat. Indeed, it is not unknown for long-lived plants to be given pet names!

Looking after houseplants requires skill and dedication because they are such a disparate group, ranging from plants native to deserts to those with a jungle heritage. Some have a limited life span, while others continue their display throughout the year.

Always check for signs of a healthy plant before you buy from a nursery or garden centre.

COMPLETE
INDOOR PLANTS

NEW HOLLAND

David Squire

First published in 2006 by New Holland Publishers Ltd.
London • Cape Town • Sydney • Auckland
• 86 Edgware Road, London W2 2EA, United Kingdom
• 80 McKenzie Street, Cape Town 8001, South Africa
• 14 Aquatic Drive, Frenchs Forest NSW 2086, Australia
• 218 Lake Road, Northcote, Auckland, New Zealand

www.newhollandpublishers.com

ISBN (HB) 1 84537 169 0
ISBN (PB) 1 84537 170 4

Publishing Managers: Claudia Dos Santos and Simon Pooley
Commissioning Editor: Alfred LeMaitre
Editor: Roxanne Reid
Designer: Lyndall du Toit
Photographer: Janet Peace, Hot Tomato Communications
Illustrators: Joy Hamilton, Bonnie Lusted
Picture Researcher: Karla Kik and Lyndall du Toit
Production: Myrna Collins
Proofreader/indexer: Elizabeth Wilson
Consultant: Jo Smith

Reproduction by Unifoto (Pty) Ltd.
Printed and bound by Times Offset (M) Sdn. Bhd., Malaysia
10 9 8 7 6 5 4 3 2 1

DISCLAIMER

Although the author and publishers have made every effort to ensure that the
information contained in this book was accurate at the time of going to press,
they accept no responsibility for any loss, injury or inconvenience sustained by
any person using this book or following the advice given in it.

BUYING HOUSEPLANTS

Choosing and buying plants for the home needs care if they are to create spectacular displays that last a long time. There are several sources of houseplants, including garden centres, nurseries, florists and high-street shops. Each has advantages, but whatever the source, it is essential to inspect the plant before buying it (*see* box on page 8).

10 tips for buying houseplants

1. Always buy from a reputable source. A cheap purchase may prove expensive if the plant dies a few weeks later.

2. Never buy a houseplant that is displayed outside a shop; in winter, such plants become chilled, while in summer they are exposed to direct, often intensive sunlight. Flowering plants suffer most from excessive cold or heat.

3. Avoid buying plants that show signs of pests and diseases (see pages 23–25). They are never a success and may infect houseplants already in your home. Check above and under leaves, as well as flowers and stems.

4. Never buy a plant with masses of roots growing out of drainage holes in the pot's base. This indicates that the plant has been neglected and needs repotting. Additionally, growth may have been retarded.

5. When buying flowering plants, ensure there are plenty of flower buds waiting to open. Avoid plants that are in full flower – their display will be short-lived.

Check there are lots of buds ready to open.

6. Do not buy plants that are wilting; this indicates neglect from which the plant may not recover.

7. Check the compost is evenly moist. Plants can wilt through excessive watering as well as from being kept dry.

This plant needs to be repotted.

Mouldy compost indicates excessive watering.

8. Avoid buying plants with green mould on the compost's surface; it indicates neglect and excessive watering.

9. Only buy clearly labelled plants, as this indicates a reputable source.

10. Do not buy large plants that are growing in very small pots, or small plants growing in very large pots. Apart from an imbalance of size and a lack of stability, large plants in small pots need frequent watering, while it is difficult to keep the moisture content of the compost of small plants in large pots even and not too wet.

The size of plants and their pots should be in balance.

Getting your plant home

The first stage in ensuring a good display is to get your plant home safely. Here are some hints.

- Either make buying a plant a separate occasion, or the last stop on a shopping expedition.
- In winter, do not put plants in a cold car boot or trunk. Also avoid these areas in summer as they quickly become excessively hot.
- Avoid putting plants in either cold or hot draughts near open windows.
- Many nurseries and garden centres sell houseplants totally covered in a paper wrapper or polythene sleeve to protect them from knocks and cold winds.
- If possible, leave young children and lively dogs at home when shopping for plants!

Protective sleeve

Acclimatizing plants to your home

As soon as possible, get your plants home and remove the wrappings. If left covered, stems and foliage may become distorted. Here are some ideas on how to establish plants indoors.

- Check the compost is lightly moist, but not saturated and waterlogged.
- Initially, place your plant in a cool or moderately warm room, out of direct and strong sunlight, and away from cold or hot draughts. After a few days, position it in its desired temperature and light intensity (*see* conditions recommended for individual plants in Part Two).
- If the plant is flowering, avoid knocking it, which may cause buds to fall off.
- If you suspect your plant is contaminated with pests and diseases, isolate and treat it with an insecticide or fungicide (*see* pages 23–25).

POTS, SAUCERS AND CACHEPOTS

These are fundamental to growing houseplants. Traditionally, pots were made of clay and these still are considered ideal for plants, though plastic pots have gained increasing popularity. Both have advantages and disadvantages.

Clay pots
- are heavier than plastic pots, creating a firm base for large plants
- have a porous nature that allows damaging salts from fertilizers to escape – a bonus if plants are excessively fed
- encourage the compost to remain cool in summer and warm in winter
- have a natural colour that harmonizes with all plants
- absorb moisture readily, so must be immersed in clean water for a few hours before use
- usually break when dropped on a hard surface
- are more difficult to clean when really dirty than plastic pots
- are more expensive than plastic pots
- are usually used in conjunction with loam-based composts

Plastic pots
- are light and easy to handle
- are not porous so plants need less frequent watering than when in clay pots
- are available in a wide colour range
- do not break easily when dropped, although cold temperatures make them brittle
- are cheaper than clay pots
- are usually used in conjunction with soil-less composts, such as those based on peat

Saucers
These are placed under pots to prevent water draining from the compost and trickling onto decorative surfaces. Most are now made of plastic, in a wide range of colours and sizes. Choose a size fractionally larger than the pot's base.

Saucers

Cachepots
Also known as cover pots and potholders, cachepots are decorative, usually complementing the decor and a plant's flowers and leaves. Some are plain colours, while others are patterned; most are round, others square. The growing pot is placed inside the cachepot. The rim of the growing pot must be level or slightly below that of the cachepot.

Cachepot

Plastic

Clay

Plastic

Clay

Match the cachepot colour to the colours of the plant.

The practical difficulty with cachepots is that it is easy unwittingly to over-water a plant. Water remains in the pot's base, eventually causing roots to decay. About 10 minutes after watering a plant, remove the plant, together with its growing pot, and tip away water remaining in the cachepot's base.

Range of pot sizes

Pots are measured by the width across the rim, ranging from 5cm (2in) to about 38cm (15in). For home gardeners who buy a plant and discard it when it ages and becomes unsightly, only a few spare pots are needed, but enthusiast houseplant growers will need a few more so plants can be repotted into larger pots. Ideally, when repotting a plant, especially when small, a pot of only about 25mm (1in) larger than the existing one is about right. However, this would require a wide assortment of pots so a range of pots, each about 5cm (2in) larger than the next, is usually selected.

POTTING COMPOSTS

Garden soil is unsuitable for growing plants in pots indoors; it has a variable nature and may contain pests, diseases and weed seeds. Buy special compost mixtures.

Traditionally, loam-based composts were – and are still – used. These are formed of partially sterilized loam, sharp sand (also known as concreting sand) and peat, with the addition of fertilizers and ground limestone or chalk. Never use soft sand (or builders' sand), which compacts when wet and does not allow air to penetrate the compost.

Difficulties in obtaining good loam encouraged the creation of composts without loam, known as soil-less composts. They are formed mainly of mixtures based on granulated peat and are uniform, as well as lighter and cleaner to use than loam-based types. Both have advantages and disadvantages.

Loam-based composts
- are heavier than peat-based types, giving greater stability to plants, especially those with a mass of foliage
- are unlikely to dry out as fast or as completely as peat-based types
- have a larger reserve of minor and trace plant foods than peat-based types
- are suitable for most houseplants

Peat-based composts
- are more uniform than loam-based composts
- are easily carried home in bags and stored (seal the bag's top by folding it over)
- are light and easy to use
- dry out more quickly than loam-based types and are more difficult to remoisten if watering is neglected
- require plants to be fed at an earlier stage in their growth than with loam-based composts

Other types of compost
The continued removal of peat from peat beds has destroyed the environments of many animals, birds, insects and native plants, so there has been pressure to use more environmentally friendly composts. These are formed of several different materials, some of which are also used as additives to other composts to help retain moisture. Look out for peat-free composts when buying soil-less types.

Specialist composts
The range of plants grown indoors is wide and it is clear that just one type of compost will not suit them all. Most flowering and foliage houseplants grow well in loam-based or peat-based composts (but do not change the type of compost when repotting a plant). Specialist plants, such as cacti and bromeliads, need types better suited to their specific needs. These can be bought from garden centres and specialist outlets.

For healthy plants, sunlight and the correct ambient temperature for the species are vital.

LIGHT AND WARMTH

Sunlight is essential for plants to grow and it must be in balance with temperature. In the wild, these are usually in harmony: as light intensity rises, so does the temperature. However, in homes – especially in winter – the temperature may be high but light intensity low. Adjustments can be made to the temperature, but this is unfortunately usually selected to suit people rather than plants.

- The intensity of light varies from one season to another, as well as throughout the day. In the plant directory in Part Two (*see* pages 38–154), the amount of light needed in winter or summer is indicated for each plant.
- Light intensity rapidly decreases as distance from a window increases. The amount of illumination at 2.4m (8ft) from a window is 5–10% of that of the light reaching a windowsill.

- Temperatures vary throughout the year; those to suit plants in winter or summer are indicated in the individual listings in Part Two.
- In general, flowering houseplants need more light than those grown mainly for their foliage, while cacti require good light at all times.
- Plants should not be moved suddenly from dull light to strong light.
- Keep windows clean, especially during winter when light intensity is low. In summer, net curtains help to diffuse strong sunlight.
- Rooms decorated in light colours reflect more light than dark shades – a major benefit in winter.
- Leaves and stems soon turn toward the light source, causing distortion. Counteract this by turning plants a quarter of a turn every few days.
- In winter, plants close to windows may receive good light but be exposed to draughts from ill-fitting window frames, causing flower buds to fall off.

THE NEED FOR WATER

Like all living things, plants are mainly formed of water and if deprived of it, eventually die. Some, such as cacti and other succulents, have water-storage mechanisms in their leaves and stems, but most plants need a regular supply. The amount required varies through the year and is influenced by light intensity and temperature.

How to judge if a plant needs water

More houseplants die each year from too little or too much water than for any other reason. Judging when to water is a skill derived from experience, although in recent years several specialized pieces of equipment have helped to take the guesswork out of this task. Year-round water requirements for individual types are indicated in the plant directory in Part Two. Here are several practical ways to judge if a plant needs water.

1. A handy 'when to water' guide is that water is needed if the surface of compost in a pot has a light colour. Conversely, when the compost is dark, it is probably sufficiently moist.

Dry compost is light in colour.

2. Place the pot, unheld, on a flat surface before tapping with a cotton-reel spiked on a bamboo cane. If this produces a ringing sound, the plant needs water; if the sound is dull and heavy, water is not required. (This technique does not work on plastic pots.)

Tap to check for dryness.

3. It is possible to use a finger to test the compost's surface, but this eventually compacts the compost.

Gently feel the compost for moisture.

4. Moisture-indicating strips – sometimes known as watering signals – can be inserted and left in the compost to indicate the need for water.

Moisture strips can be helpful.

5. Moisture meters (devices for assessing the moisture in compost) are accurate but involve inserting a spiked probe into the compost and getting a reading on a dial. Doing this repeatedly damages roots.

Moisture meters are accurate.

Watering a houseplant

There are several ways to water a houseplant. The usual method is 'over the rim'. This involves using an indoor watering can to pour water into the space between the top of the compost and the rim of the pot. Allow water to seep into the compost and drain through it, into a saucer. After about 10 minutes, tip away excess water from the saucer.

Alternatively, where it is essential not to moisten the leaves (especially those that are hairy and soft, such as saintpaulias and *Episcia cupreata*), stand the pot in a bowl shallowly filled with water. When moisture rises to the compost's surface, remove the plant and pot and allow excess water to drain.

Saving a plant with exceptionally dry compost

Sometimes, compost becomes exceptionally dry, especially if watering is neglected in summer or during holidays.

* If neglect is only superficial, stand the plant on a well-drained surface and water the compost two or three times. At each watering, the compost expands and makes it better able to retain moisture when further water is applied.
* Where a plant is dramatically wilting, remove dead flowers and leaves and stand the plant in a bowl shallowly filled with water. When water seeps to the surface of the compost, remove the plant and allow excess moisture to drain.

Rescuing a plant with wet compost

In winter, when houseplants are usually not growing rapidly, plants are sometimes excessively watered, resulting in leaves and flowers wilting. If the compost is not totally saturated, there is a good chance of rescuing it.

With the plant still in its pot, support the compost with one hand and invert the plant and pot. Remove the pot. Use an absorbent cloth or kitchen towel to soak up excess moisture – repeated wrappings are usually needed. Leave the soil-ball wrapped in absorbent paper until dry, but not bone-dry. If the root-ball is packed with roots that hold it together, omit the wrapping. When the compost is only slightly moist, repot the root-ball into a clean pot.

Water the compost and allow to drain.

Place plants that do not like getting their leaves wet in a bowl of water to absorb water from below.

Wilting can be the result of excessive watering.

Stand a plant with dry compost in a bowl of water.

Type of water

Most houseplant enthusiasts use tap water, which suits the majority of plants. It is clean and readily available, and it is ideal as long as it is not too cold. However, houseplants such as azaleas dislike lime and grow best in slightly acid soil. If the tap water is alkaline, boil it and allow it to stand until cool before use. Collecting defrosted iced water from a refrigerator and allowing it to reach room temperature is another option.

Rainwater is ideal, but ensure that it is clean and has not fallen on a dirt-contaminated roof or become stagnant in a barrel.

Rescuing and repotting a plant with wet compost

1. Remove the pot.
2. Soak up excess moisture.
3. Wrap and leave to dry out.
4. Repot into a clean pot when the compost is only slightly moist.

HUMIDITY AND MIST-SPRAYING

The amount of humidity in the air influences the health and growth of plants. Desert cacti and most other succulents survive in areas with little humidity, but plants native to forests usually need a humid atmosphere.

How to create humidity around plants

1. Stand plants in small groups to create a humid mini-environment.
2. Stand pots in trays with a 25mm (1in) layer of pebbles in the base, shallowly filled with water to just below the top of the pebbles. Moist air can then rise around the leaves.
3. Use a mist-sprayer, which is inexpensive, to coat the leaves in fine water droplets, but do not spray flowers or plants with hairy leaves.
4. Mist-spray plants in the morning, so moisture can evaporate before night. Dampness remaining on the leaves in late evening encourages the presence of diseases at night when the temperature falls.

5. Mist-spray aerial roots, such as those on *Monstera deliciosa* and some Philodendrons, to help them to remain soft, pliable and active.
6. Avoid spraying plants when they are in strong, direct sunlight; water droplets may act as lenses and burn the leaves.
7. Regular mist-spraying helps to discourage red spider mite infestation.

Signs of excessive humidity

- Leaves and flowers that are tightly packed together sometimes become excessively damp.
- Flower petals and buds eventually become covered in a furry mould.
- Soft, hairy leaves become damaged before shiny, all-green ones.
- Cacti and other succulents develop patches of decay.
- Plants with leaves that clasp stems become damaged; water becomes trapped at the junctions of leaf-stalks and leaves.

Signs of an excessively dry atmosphere

- Tips of leaves become curled, dry and shrivelled.
- Flowers fade and become discoloured, with flower buds eventually falling off.
- Tips of shoots wilt and, later, shrivel.
- Surfaces of leaves become dull.
- The whole plant wilts if the temperature is high, with leaves eventually falling off.

REPOTTING HOUSEPLANTS

Eventually, most houseplants (except those grown for their short-term display) fill their pots with roots and need to be transferred to slightly larger ones. A plant left in the same pot will slowly deteriorate. When selecting a new pot check the following.

- The new pot is clean, dry and about 25mm (1in) larger. When a plant is already in a large pot, perhaps 15cm (6in) or more wide, the new pot can be 5cm (2in) larger.
- When repotting into a clay pot, put a piece of broken clay pot (known as a crock), concave side downward, in the base to prevent the drainage hole becoming blocked. This is unnecessary when repotting into plastic pots; these are usually filled with peat-based compost, which is more fibrous and less likely to fall out of the smaller drainage holes into the base.
- Use the same type of compost in which the plant is already growing.

Use a cachepot or place the pot on a saucer after repotting.

Step-by-step to repotting

1. The day before repotting, thoroughly water the compost and allow the excess to drain. This is essential since a plant with a dry root-ball will not rapidly become established in a new pot.
2. Place the fingers of one hand over the top of the root-ball and invert it, together with the pot. Sharply tap the rim on a hard surface (without damaging the plant's leaves), so the pot and root-ball separate.
3. Fill a suitable pot with compost to about one-third of its depth and lightly firm it. First, add a crock in its base if it is a clay pot.
4. Without damaging the root-ball, position it in the centre of the pot. Check that the top of the root-ball is about 12mm (½in) below the new pot's rim. Add or remove compost.
5. Keep the plant and root-ball upright and carefully dribble fresh compost around it. Gently firm it until just covering the root-ball. When repotting a plant in a large pot, leave a slightly larger space between the compost's surface and rim.
6. Stand the plant on a well-drained surface and gently water the compost from above, without unduly disturbing it. A couple of waterings may be necessary. Watering from above also helps to settle fresh compost around the root-ball.
7. Stand the pot on a clean saucer or place it in a cachepot. Initially, position the plant in light shade for two to three days, or until established.

FEEDING

To remain healthy, plants need a balanced diet throughout their lives. For most, this is provided by compost in a pot, with the addition of regular feeding or, for plants in large pots, top-dressing.

Regular feeding makes a remarkable difference and there are three main ways to do this.

- **Liquid fertilizers** are the traditional, easiest and most widely used choice for feeding houseplants. Concentrated fertilizers are diluted in clean water and applied to potting composts. First read the instructions and add the correct amount to clean water. Agitate and apply to moist compost. Many bromeliads have urns at their centres (resembling small vases formed by leaves); keep these topped up with water, and add weak liquid fertilizer, usually from spring to late summer.

- **Fertilizer pills and sticks** are more recent innovations. They are pushed into the compost to provide food for several months. They are best used in spring and up to midsummer. If they are used in late summer, they provide food when some plants are resting. Unfortunately, unlike liquid feeding

Dilute liquid fertilizer in water and stir.

Apply liquid fertilizer to moist compost.

Add weak liquid fertlilizer to a bromeliad's central urn.

Insert a fertilizer stick into the compost.

To prevent fertilizer from going all over the place when you foliar feed plants, simply place the plants in a plastic bag.

(which encourages the development of roots throughout the compost), pills and sticks concentrate nutrients in one position, resulting in an uneven spread of roots.

- **Foliar feeds** are ideal for houseplants that can absorb nutrients through their leaves. Air-plants are normally fed in this way. Plants rapidly respond to foliar feeding and the technique is best used as a tonic for plants with smooth, non-hairy leaves. Avoid spraying flowers or using foliar feeds when plants are in strong sunlight. Strong foliar feeds will burn the leaves.

Remember that not all houseplants need feeding at the same frequency throughout the year. While most are fed during summer, not all need feeding in winter (*see* the plant directory in Part Two for details). Before feeding a plant, check that the compost is moist; this decreases the risk of roots becoming burned by strong chemicals and helps spread plant foods throughout the compost.

Feeds that are too strong soon damage roots, so it is essential to adhere to the manufacturer's instructions. To avoid root damage, it is better to provide a plant with a weak liquid fertilizer than one that is too strong.

Top-dressing large houseplants

Instead of being repotted, large plants are usually top-dressed.

1. Use a small trowel to carefully remove the surface compost without damaging the roots. The depth of the compost that is removed is usually no more than 25mm (1in).

2. Add slow-release fertilizer to fresh compost and use it to top up the pot so its surface is about 12mm (½in) below the rim. Then, carefully water the compost using a watering-can with a rose.

GROOMING AND SUPPORTING

Grooming keeps houseplants attractive throughout their lives. Flowering houseplants need to have dead flowers removed, while others need to be supported or to have their leaves cleaned. When removing dead flowers and leaves, put them into a bag and throw them away; do not scatter them around a plant because decaying pieces of plants are unsightly and encourage the presence of diseases.

Wipe the leaf with a damp cloth to restore shine and remove dust.

Cleaning leaves

Houseplants with large leaves, such as the Rubber Plant (*Ficus elastica*), benefit from having them cleaned. Dust and dirt left on leaves impairs their appearance and prevents sunlight from activating growth processes.

- Use a soft, damp cloth to clean large, shiny leaves. Support the leaf with one hand and carefully wipe the surface. To avoid burning, never do this when the plant is in strong sunlight.
- If a plant has a large number of small, shiny leaves, gently swirl them in a bowl filled with slightly warm water. When clean, remove the plant and stand it away from direct sunlight until dry or it might burn.
- Use a soft brush to gently remove dust from hairy leaves. Blowing on leaves while brushing them helps to remove dust.

Swirl leaves under water to rinse off dust and dirt.

Tidying stems and shoots

- Some plants become untidy and benefit from having stems and shoots removed. Where a stem or shoot spoils a plant's symmetry, use sharp scissors to cut it back to just above a leaf-joint. Avoid leaving small stubs, which are unsightly and will die back.

Use a paint brush to clean dust off hairy leaves.

- Young foliage plants often need to have a shoot tip removed to encourage bushiness. Use sharp scissors to cut back the stem to a leaf-joint, or hold the shoot between your fingers and snap it sideways.
- Some variegated plants occasionally produce all-green stems; cut these off.

Trim off untidy long growth with a sharp pair of scissors.

For houseplants with long flower stems, break off from the base of the stem to discourage disease.

Snap off dead flowers between your thumb and forefinger.

Removing dead flowers

Dead flowers are unsightly and encourage the presence of diseases if left on a plant. Most dead flowers are removed by pinching them off between a finger and thumb. For houseplants such as cyclamen, remove the complete flower stem and dead flower; leaving short pieces of stem encourages the presence of diseases. Gently tug the stem so it parts from the plant's base.

Staking and supporting

When plants need to be supported it is essential that this is unobtrusive, whether you use traditional materials (raffia, green string and split canes) or more recent introductions (plastic frameworks and metal rings).

- Most houseplants need little support, but if this becomes necessary use a thin split cane and soft green string. First tie the string to the support, then loop it around the stem just below a leaf-joint. Metal plant rings can also be used.
- Some climbing plants, such as *Jasminum polyanthum* (Pink Jasmine), benefit from a supporting hoop formed of pliable canes. When the plant is young and has shoots about 30cm (12in) long, insert pliable canes into the compost and train the stems around the canes.
- Climbing plants with aerial roots benefit from being given a moss pole as support (this is a stiff stake covered with several layers of moss). Use spirals of green string to hold it in position. Tie the plant's stems to the pole and keep the moss damp.

Form a hoop with pliable cane and attach plant with string.

Right: A moss pole works well as a support for a climbing plant with aerial roots.

Holiday care

Invariably, there are times when plants are left unattended for several days. This is not a problem in winter, when most are not very active, but arrangements need to be made to look after them in summer.

Helping plants survive

1. If you are going away for only a few days, place a plastic sheet on the floor in the centre of a room and stand your plants on it. Fill their saucers with water.
2. Keep small plants moist by standing them in a shallow tray packed with moist peat.
3. Place a piece of capillary matting on a draining board and trail the other end into a sink full of water. Stand plants directly on it, not in their saucers. This works well for plants growing in peat-based compost in plastic pots, without crocks in their base.

4. Use wicks to keep compost moist in small pots. Push a wick into the compost and trail the other end into a pot filled with water.

Use wicks to water plants.

5. Shallowly fill a wide washing-up bowl with clean water and place one or more plants in it. This is ideal for houseplants that like plenty of moisture, such as some ferns.

Stand plants in a bowl of water.

6. Fill a shallow container with expanded clay particles, add water to just below the surface and stand the plants on top.

Before leaving home

1. Close the door of the room to prevent draughts drying plants, or pets knocking them over.
2. Draw curtains in summer, especially those that face strong, direct sunlight.
3. A week before leaving home, check that plants are not infested with pests and diseases. Spray immediately if they are.
4. Remove faded flowers and those that will be past their best by the time you return. Remove dead leaves.

Remove faded flowers.

Stand plants on capillary matting.

Remove dead leaves.

HOUSEPLANT PROBLEMS

Few plants can escape from pests and diseases, or cultural problems (often known as physiological disorders), such as leaves and flower buds falling off. It is much easier to prevent attack by pests and diseases than to eliminate them from badly affected plants. Here are some prevention tips.

- Buy plants from reputable sources.
- Inspect plants before buying.
- Regularly check for infestations.
- Never use garden soil instead of potting compost as it may contain weed seeds, pests or diseases.
- Avoid leaving dead flowers and leaves around plants.
- Check root-balls for soil pests when plants are being repotted.
- Never use infected plants as propagation material.

The chemicals permitted by legislation vary from country to country and state to state so if prevention fails, check with your local nursery or garden centre about the most suitable insecticide to use for your specific problem.

PESTS

Aphids: also known as greenfly, aphis and aphides, they are the main pests of houseplants. These small, usually green, sap-sucking insects infest flowers, shoot tips and soft leaves, sucking sap and causing mottling and distortion. They also excrete honeydew, which attracts ants and encourages the presence of the fungal disease, sooty mould.
Control: spray with a suitable insecticide as soon as aphids are seen. Repeat every 10–14 days throughout summer.

Cyclamen mites: these infest a wide range of plants, including cyclamen, pelargoniums, saintpaulias (African Violets) and impatiens (Busy Lizzies). They are minute, eight-legged, spider-like creatures that cluster on the under-

PESTS

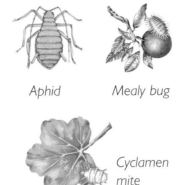

Aphid   Mealy bug

Cyclamen mite

Red spider mite

Vine weevil

Scale insect

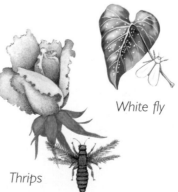

White fly

Thrips

sides of leaves. They suck sap, causing leaves to crinkle and darken. Flowering is shortened and buds become distorted and may fall off.
Control: remove and burn seriously infested leaves and flowers. Spray with an acaricide. Destroy badly infected plants to prevent the mites spreading.

Mealy bugs: white, waxy, woodlice-like creatures that live in groups and especially infest ferns, palms, azaleas and hippeastrums. They suck sap, causing distortion, loss of vigour and yellowing of leaves. They excrete honeydew, which encourages the presence of ants and sooty mould.
Control: wipe off light infestations with cotton-buds dipped into methylated spirits (rubbing alcohol). Spray with a suitable insecticide or burn seriously infected plants.

Red spider mites: also known as greenhouse red spider mites, they are spider-like, minute, usually red, and have eight legs. They suck leaves, causing mottling and, if the infestation is severe, webs. These are unsightly, reduce air circulation around the plant and make eradication difficult.
Control: mist-spray daily with clean water (but avoid spraying flowers or soft leaves) and spray with a suitable acaricide.

Scale insects: swollen, waxy-brown discs, usually static, under which female scale insects produce their young.
Control: young scale insects can be wiped away with a cotton-bud dipped in methylated spirits (rubbing alcohol). Established colonies are difficult to eradicate and badly contaminated plants are best burned.

Thrips: these tiny, dark-brown, fly-like insects jump from one plant to another. They pierce leaves and flowers, sucking sap and causing silvery mottling and

streaking. Undersides of leaves develop small globules of a red liquid that eventually turns black.
Control: spray several times with a suitable insecticide or burn seriously infected plants. Keep the compost moist because dryness intensifies the damage caused by these insects.

Vine weevils: serious pests in the adult form, when young and as larvae. Adults are beetle-like, with a short snout. They chew all parts of plants. The larvae – fat, legless and creamy-white, with brown heads – inhabit compost and chew roots.
Control: immediately water compost with suitable insecticide and spray leaves. Destroy badly infected plants.

Whitefly: small, moth-like white insects that flutter from one plant to another when disturbed. They have a mealy or powder-like covering and are mostly found on the undersides of leaves, sucking sap, causing distortion and excreting honeydew, which encourages the presence of ants and sooty mould.
Control: eradication is not easy; several sprayings at five-day intervals with a suitable insecticide are essential.

DISEASES
Black leg: a disease mainly of cuttings, especially of pelargoniums; the bases become black and soft.
Control: this is encouraged by cold, wet, airless compost so ensure compost is well aerated when taking cuttings. If cuttings are infected, they are best removed and destroyed; for rare or unusual varieties, remove cuttings, cut off the blacked area and reinsert the base in fresh compost.

Botrytis: also known as grey mould, it attacks soft parts of plants, such as flowers, young leaves and shoots, covering them with a grey, furry mould.
Control: cut off and destroy infected parts. Spray infected plants with a suitable

DISEASES

Black leg

Botrytis

Damping off

Powdery mildew

Rust

Sooty mould

Virus

fungicide. Remove dead flowers to discourage spreading. Avoid damp, still air and excessive water.

Damping off: attacks seedlings soon after they germinate, causing them to turn black and collapse.
Control: sow seeds thinly in well-drained compost and place in a warm and well-aerated position. Avoid excessively watering the compost.

Powdery mildew: fungal disease that produces a white, powdery coating. It usually appears in spring and summer, infecting leaves, flowers and stems.
Control: remove badly infected leaves, stems and flowers; increase ventilation and keep the atmosphere dry.

Rusts: complex diseases that are more problematic in sunrooms and conservatories than indoors. They produce raised rings of brown or black spots. Plants become unsightly and lose their vigour.
Control: remove and burn infected plants and increase ventilation. Do not propagate from infected plants.

Sooty mould: black, fungal disease that grows on leaves, stems and flowers covered with honeydew (*see* aphids and other sap-sucking insects). At first it appears in small clusters, but later covers the entire surface.
Control: spray with a suitable insecticide against sap-sucking insects. Use a damp cloth to remove the black growth from leaves. Flowers are best cut off.

Viruses: microscopic particles that invade plants (and animals), causing disorders in the tissue but seldom immediately killing their host.
Control: regularly spray with a suitable insecticide against sap-sucking insects (which probably introduced the problem to your plants) and burn badly infected plants.

Non-chemical control of pests and diseases

Apart from growing plants healthily, with adequate moisture, food and circulation of air, there are other ways to keep them healthy and to ward off pests and diseases.

1. Mist-spray plants with clean water where there is a risk (or presence) of red spider mites.
2. Regularly remove dead leaves and flowers.
3. Use insecticidal soaps, which are ideal against a wide range of insects and mites.
4. Investigate biological controls, which means using other insects and mites to control pests. These are especially suitable where insects have developed resistance to chemical controls. Biological controls exist for aphids, caterpillars, mealy bugs, soft scale insects, red spider mites, thrips, vine weevil larvae and whiteflies. Ask your garden centre for advice.

CULTURAL PROBLEMS

Also known as physiological disorders, these are not caused by pests or diseases but by environmental problems.

Wilting: there are several causes, including too much water, too little water, and the result of soil pests that eat and destroy roots. Usually, plants wilt because they are short of water; if the compost is dry, water the plant several times. Alternatively, stand the plant, in its pot, in a bowl of water. Later, remove and allow excess water to drain. If a plant wilts and the compost is exceptionally wet, remove the pot and dry the root-ball (*see* page 15).

Leaves fall off: occasionally, leaves fall off as a result of factors such as dry or wet soil, pests and disease, and cultural influences, including a sudden drop in temperature. Reposition the plant and keep it in an even, warm temperature away from draughts. Leaves that become yellow and gradually drop off are the result of excessive watering or inadequate feeding.

Flower buds fall off: this may happen if the plant is in a draught, a dry atmosphere or has received a sudden chill. Buds often drop off if a plant is severely knocked.

Damaged leaf surfaces: lack of water may make the edges of leaves become crisp and brown, but straw-coloured patches on leaves, especially soft and hairy ones, are the result of water splashing on the surface, which is then burnt by strong sunlight.

Applying chemicals

There are several ways in which insecticides and fungicides can be applied to plants.

1. **Spraying** is the most common method. One way to treat a plant in a small house or apartment is to put it in a large plastic bag, which can be temporarily sealed after spraying is complete.
2. **Dusting** is popular and a puffer-type applicator is readily available.
3. **Insecticidal sticks** are pushed into the compost. The plant's roots absorb the chemical and the whole plant becomes toxic to insects.

Safety tips

1. Follow the manufacturer's instructions and never use stronger or weaker solutions.
2. Unless recommended, never mix two different chemicals.
3. Check the chemical is suitable for the plants being sprayed – some plants are susceptible to specific chemicals.
4. Store chemicals away from children and household pets.
5. Avoid spraying if animals are in the room; fish and birds are especially harmed by chemical sprays.
6. Never allow children or animals to lick or chew plants that have been sprayed.
7. Only apply chemicals suitable for use indoors. This will be indicated on the label, but if in doubt, ask your nursery or garden centre for advice.

INCREASING HOUSEPLANTS

There are several easy ways to increase your houseplants and for a few of them very little equipment is needed. Some methods produce many new plants, while in others just one new plant is created, such as when air-layering a Ficus elastica *(Rubber Plant).*

SOWING SEEDS

Many houseplants can be increased from seeds. If you want several plants of the same type, this is a relatively inexpensive method. Bear in mind, though, that equipment such as seed-trays, pots and compost are needed, as well as a greenhouse, sunroom or conservatory where gentle warmth can be provided.

Step-by-step: sowing seeds
1. If only a few seeds are to be sown, use a small, shallow pot, but a plastic seed-tray is better for larger numbers. Fill it with seed compost and use your fingers to firm it, especially around the edges.

2. Place more compost in the seed-tray and use a straight-edged piece of wood to level it with the rim. Then, use a flat-surfaced compost firmer to firm the compost to 12mm (½in) below the rim so seeds can be lightly covered and watered without water spilling out.

3. Tip a few seeds into a piece of light-coloured, stiff paper folded into a V-shape. Then gently tap its end to distribute seeds evenly over the surface, but not within 12mm (½in) of the edges.

4. Use a flat-based horticultural sieve to cover the seeds in seed compost to about three times their thickness. Alternatively, use a culinary sieve.

5. Shallowly fill a bowl with clean water and stand the seed-tray in it until moisture seeps to the surface. Remove and allow excess water to drain.

6. Cover the seed-tray with a clear plastic lid to prevent the compost's surface from drying out and to help maintain a gently warm temperature. Wipe the inside of the cover every day to remove condensation. Remove it entirely when seedlings germinate and small seed leaves can be seen.

Houseplants raised from seeds

Many houseplants can be raised from seeds – from foliage and flowering plants to palms, cacti and other succulents. The following are just a few popular examples of seed-raised plants, but there are many others.

Flowering houseplants
Begonia semperflorens (Wax Begonia)
Calceolaria x *herbeohybrida* (Slipper Plant)
Cyclamen persicum (Cyclamen)
Exacum affine (Persian Violet)
Impatiens walleriana (Busy Lizzie)
Kalanchoe blossfeldiana (Flaming Katy)
Primula malacoides (Fairy Primrose)
Schizanthus pinnatus (Butterfly Flower)
Senecio cruentus (Cineraria)

Foliage houseplants
Coleus blumei (Flame Nettle)
Grevillea robusta (Silky Oak)

Palms for the home
Chamaedorea elegans (Parlour Palm)
Chamaedorea seifrizii (Reed Palm)
Howea forsteriana (Kentia Palm)

STEM-TIP CUTTINGS

Dibber

TAKING CUTTINGS

Many houseplants can be increased from cuttings. There are several different types of cuttings, but most important is that they should be healthy and free from pests and diseases.

Step-by-step: stem-tip cuttings
Each cutting is formed of a piece of stem, several leaves and a terminal shoot. They are usually 7.5–10cm (3–4in) long and, if possible, taken from the outer parts of a mother plant, where they have received good light and are growing healthily and strongly.

1. Use a sharp knife to sever a healthy shoot close to the parent plant (do not leave a short stub).

2. Also use a sharp, clean knife to prepare the cutting, cutting just below a leaf-joint. Then cut off the lower leaves.

3. Fill a small pot with equal parts moist peat and sharp sand and firm it to 12mm (½in) below the rim. Use a small dibber to form a hole into which the stem can be inserted about 25mm (1in) deep. Firm compost around the stem and lightly water from above.

4. Insert 3–4 short split canes into the compost and cover with a plastic bag. Use an elastic band to secure the bag around the pot. When shoots develop, remove the bag. Later, when growing strongly, transfer the rooted cutting to another pot.

Step-by-step: leaf-stem cuttings

Leaf-stem cuttings resemble stem-tip cuttings, but without the tip. This is an excellent way to increase plants with long, trailing stems, which have leaves at regular intervals. Examples include both variegated and all-green forms of *Hedera helix* (Common Ivy).

1. Select a long, healthy stem from a mother plant and sever it just above a leaf. Do not use old, hard stems.

2. Cut the stem to form several cuttings; cut just above a leaf, so that each cutting is formed of a leaf and piece of stem about 36mm (1½in) long. The stem part can be shortened if too long.

3. Fill a pot with equal parts moist peat and sharp sand and firm to 12mm (½in) below the rim. Use a dibber to insert 3–4 cuttings in each pot, each 18–25mm (¾–1in) deep, spaced out but not less than 12mm (½in) from the pot's side. Firm compost around their bases and gently water from above.

4. Insert 3–4 short split canes into the compost and cover with a plastic bag secured around the pot with an elastic band. When shoots develop, remove the bag. Cuttings can be separated and repotted individually, but to produce a display more quickly just repot the entire pot of cuttings into another pot.

Step-by-step: leaf-petiole cuttings

Often used to increase *Saintpaulia ionantha* (African Violet), this involves cuttings formed of a leaf and a small stalk (petiole).

1. Form each cutting by severing the stem of a healthy leaf at the base of a mother plant, but avoid leaving short spurs or stems.

2. Use a sharp knife to trim back stems to about 36mm (1½in) long.

3. Fill a small pot with equal parts moist peat and sharp sand; firm to 12mm (½in) below the rim. Dip the end of each cutting in hormone rooting powder and use a small dibber to insert it so the base of the leaf is just above the compost. Firm compost around the stem and lightly water from above. Several cuttings can be inserted in each pot and tranferred to individual pots when they develop small shoots.

LEAF-STEM CUTTINGS

LEAF-PETIOLE CUTTINGS

WHOLE-LEAF CUTTINGS

1

2

3

4

5 & 6

LEAF-SQUARE CUTTINGS

1

2

3 & 4

Step-by-step: whole-leaf cuttings

Large-leaved begonias, such as *Begonia rex* (Rex Begonia) and *Begonia masoniana* (Iron Cross Begonia), can be increased by this method or the one below.

1. The day before taking cuttings, water the mother plant so leaves are full of moisture. Select a healthy leaf and sever its stem just above the plant's base.

2. Invert the leaf and use a sharp knife to sever the stem close to the underside of the leaf.

3. Cut across main veins on the leaf's underside with a sharp knife, positioning cuts 18–25mm ($^3\!/_4$–1in) apart. Do not cut completely through the leaf.

4. Fill a seed-tray with equal amounts moist peat and sharp sand; firm it to 12mm ($^1\!/_2$in) below the rim. Place the leaf on the compost vein-side downward and lightly press it down, holding in position with a few pebbles (or use U-shaped pieces of wire).

5. Put a plastic cover over the seed-tray and place in gentle warmth. Keep the compost lightly moist.

6. Later, when small plants develop from the leaf's surface, these can be moved to individual pots.

Step-by-step: leaf-square cuttings

1. Cut a healthy leaf from a parent plant and sever the stem close to the leaf's underside. Position the leaf upside down and cut it into 3cm (1¼in) square pieces. Each must have several veins.

2. Fill a seed-tray with equal parts moist peat and sharp sand; firm to 12mm ($^1\!/_2$in) below the rim. For each leaf cutting, use the blade of a knife to form a slit about 12mm ($^1\!/_2$in) deep in the compost's surface. Push the side of a cutting (which was nearest to the leaf stalk) into the slit and firm compost around it.

3. Insert other leaf cuttings – not within 12mm ($^1\!/_2$in) of the edge – and gently water from above without disturbing the cuttings. Allow excess moisture to drain, then cover with a plastic dome.

4. When young shoots develop from each cutting, transfer them to individual pots.

Step-by-step: leaf-triangle cuttings

This is another popular way to increase large-leaved houseplants. As with leaf-square cuttings, several new plants can be produced from one leaf.

1. Cut a healthy leaf from a parent plant and sever the stem close to the leaf's underside. Leave the leaf upside down and cut it into triangles, which tend to be longer than the squares of leaf-square cuttings (*see* page 29). These can be inserted deeper into the compost, which helps to give them greater stability.

2. Fill a seed-tray with equal parts moist peat and sharp sand; firm to 12mm (½in) below the rim. Use a knife to form a slit 18–25mm (¾–1in) deep in the compost's surface. Push the end of a cutting (which was nearest to the leaf-stalk) into the slit and firm compost around it.

3. Insert other leaf cuttings (not within 12mm (½in) of the side) and gently water from above without disturbing the cuttings. Allow excess moisture to drain, then cover with a plastic dome.

4. When young shoots develop from each cutting, transfer them to individual pots.

Step-by-step: cross-leaf cuttings

Sometimes known as cross-section and leaf-section cuttings, this technique is often used to increase *Streptocarpus* x *hybridus* (Cape Primrose).

1. The day before taking cuttings, water the mother plant and allow excess water to drain. Sever a healthy leaf close to the base, place on a board and cut into cross-sections 5cm (2in) wide.

2. Fill a seed-tray with equal parts moist peat and sharp sand; firm to 12mm (½in) below the rim. With a sharp knife, form slits 18mm (¾in) deep. Insert the cutting's base into the slit. Firm compost around it.

3. Gently water the compost. Allow the leaf's surface to dry and place a transparent lid on top. When young shoots develop from the leaf, detach them individually (usually with part of the parent leaf still attached) and transfer them to a small pot. Small but established cuttings have a better chance of being repotted successfully than large ones.

LEAF-TRIANGLE CUTTINGS

CROSS-LEAF CUTTINGS

HORIZONTAL CANE CUTTINGS

1

2

3

4

VERTICAL CANE CUTTINGS

1

2

3

Step-by-step: horizontal cane cuttings

Several thick-stemmed houseplants can be increased in this way, including dieffenbachias (Dumb Cane), dracaenas and cordylines.

1. Water the mother plant the day before taking cuttings. Sever a strong, healthy stem at its base, trying not to spoil the plant's shape.

2. Use a sharp knife to cut the stem into 5–7.5cm (2–3in) long pieces; each part must have at least one strong bud (they grow from leaf joints).

3. Fill a pot, 13cm (5in) wide, with equal parts moist peat and sharp sand; firm to 12mm (½in) below the rim. Press each cutting horizontally into compost to half its thickness, with the strongest bud facing upward. Hold in place with pieces of U-shaped wire.

4. Lightly water the compost, allow excess to drain and cover with a plastic lid. When shoots and roots develop, transfer them to individual pots.

Step-by-step: vertical cane cuttings

Several houseplants can be increased in this way, including yuccas and dracaenas. Sometimes these cuttings are known as Ti-log cuttings (a word of Polynesian derivation), although properly this name refers solely to *Cordyline fruticosa*, earlier known as *Cordyline terminalis* and *Dracaena terminalis*. These Ti-logs are widely sold as specially prepared cuttings, with ends covered in wax. The following advice refers specifically to them.

1. Cut off wax from the lower end, but leave the wax covering the top intact, as this prevents loss of moisture before the cutting forms roots.

2. Add a handful of equal parts moist peat and sharp to the base of a pot. Hold the cutting with the waxed end upward and pot it up so its base is 36–50mm (1½–2in) deep. Gently water the compost.

3. To encourage rapid rooting, put the pot and cutting in an opaque bag and place in gentle warmth. Check the compost every 10 days to ensure it is still damp. When shoots appear, remove the bag and slowly acclimatize the plant to a lower temperature. Later, usually in 2–4 weeks, transfer the rooted cutting to a larger pot.

Step-by-step: cactus cuttings

Some cacti, especially those that form clusters, can be increased from cuttings taken in spring or early summer. Remember to wear gloves when taking these cuttings.

1. Use a sharp knife to sever a few stems from the plant's base, taking care not to spoil its shape. Allow cut ends to dry for a day or so, then insert in compost.

2. Fill a small pot with equal parts moist peat and sharp sand; firm to 12mm (½in) below the rim. Use a small dibber to form a hole to a depth about one-third of the cutting's length. Insert the cutting, firm the compost and lightly water from above. When young shoots develop or fresh growth develops at the cutting's top, transfer to an individual pot.

Step-by-step: small-leaved succulent cuttings

Several succulents, such as echeverias and crassulas, have small leaves that can be removed and encouraged to develop roots.

1. Water the mother plant the day before taking cuttings. Select a healthy leaf and gently snap it off downward or sideways. Take several cuttings without spoiling the plant's shape. Allow cut edges to dry for a day or so.

2. Fill a pot with equal parts moist peat and sharp sand; firm to 12mm (½in) below the rim. Add a dusting of sharp sand to the surface. Use a small dibber or knife to insert each cutting to about one-third of its length.

3. When young shoots and roots develop from a cutting's base, it can be transferred to another pot.

DIVIDING

Dividing is a quick and easy way to increase houseplants with fibrous roots and several stems. Spring and early summer are the best times to divide them.

Step-by-step: division

1. The day before dividing a congested plant, water the compost and allow excess to drain. Then, to divide, place a hand over the soil-ball and invert the pot. Sharply tap the pot's rim on a hard surface so the pot and root-ball separate.

CACTUS CUTTINGS

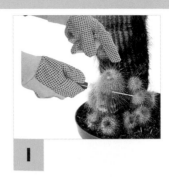

1

2

SMALL-LEAVED SUCCULENT CUTTINGS

1

2

3

DIVIDING

1

2. Place the root-ball on a firm surface and gently tease it apart into several substantial-sized pieces, making certain that each part has healthy roots, stems and leaves.

3. Prepare a clean, dry pot, filling its base with compost. Position one of the new plants centrally in the pot, so that the base of the stems is about 12mm (½in) below the rim. Dribble compost around the roots, firming it in layers until 12mm (½in) below the rim. Tap the side of the rim to level the compost.

4. Water the plant from above by using a watering can with a fine rose. This helps to settle compost around the roots of the newly divided plants. Place the plant in a lightly shaded position until it is established. By dividing a congested plant, several new plants can be produced.

Houseplants suitable for dividing

Aspidistra elatior (Aspidistra)
Calathea makoyana (Peacock Plant) and other calatheas
Chlorophytum comosum (Spider Plant)
Ctenanthe oppenheimiana tricolor (Never-never Plant)

Cyperus alternifolius (Umbrella Grass)
Ferns (many can be divided)
Fittonia argyroneura (Silver Net Plant) and other fittonias
Maranta leuconeura (Prayer Plant) and other marantas

Saintpaulia ionantha (African Violet)
Sansevieria trifasciata var. laurentii (Mother-in-law's Tongue)
Soleirolia soleirolii (Mind Your Own Business)
Spathiphyllum wallisii (Peace Lily)

LAYERING

LAYERING

This is an easy way to increase houseplants with pliable stems, such as those that trail or climb. Late spring and early summer are the best times to do this.

Step-by-step: layering
1. The day before layering a plant, water the compost to ensure stems are turgid. Allow excess moisture to drain. Fill a clean pot, firming moist peat and sharp sand to about 12mm (½in) below the rim.

2. Bend a long stem near a leaf stalk and about 13cm (5in) from its end. This bend is not meant to sever the stem, but to constrict it so roots will develop at that point.

3. Use a small piece of U-shaped wire to secure the bent section of stem 25–36mm (1–1½in) deep in the compost. Firm compost around and over the stem and lightly water it.

4. Put the mother plant and the layered stem in a plastic tray, so that they can be moved together. When fresh shoots develop, use a sharp knife to sever the stem.

Houseplants suitable for layering

Epipremnum aureum (Devil's Ivy)
Hedera canariensis 'Variegata' (Canary Island Ivy)
Hedera helix (Common Ivy): there are many variegated forms
Philodendron scandens (Sweetheart Plant)

Air-layering

Air-layering is used to increase large, woody house-plants such as *Ficus elastica* (Rubber Plant) that have grown tall, with bare woody stems. Best undertaken in early and midsummer, it involves partially severing a stem just below the lowest leaf and encouraging it to develop roots.

Step by step: air-layering a Rubber Plant
1. Choose a healthy plant that is bare of leaves on the lower part of its stem. The top 45cm (1½ft) of the plant should have healthy leaves.

2. Use a sharp knife to make an upward-slanting cut, two-thirds through the stem and 7.5–10cm (3–4in) below the lowest leaf. Take care that the top part does not snap off.

3. Insert a matchstick into the cut to hold it open. Trim off its ends and use a small brush to coat the cut surfaces with a hormone rooting powder.

AIR-LAYERING A RUBBER PLANT

4. Wind a piece of clear polythene film, about 23cm (9in) wide and 30cm (12in) long, around the stem and secure its base about 5cm (2in) below the cut.

5. Fill the tube formed by the polythene with moist peat. Firm it to about 7.5cm (3in) below the tube's top. Tie the top around the stem with string.

6. Keep compost in the pot moist so the plant continues to grow. Six to eight weeks later you will see through the polythene that roots have formed.

7. Hold the top of the plant and sever the stem directly below the polythene. Carefully remove the film.

8. Immediately pot up the plant into potting compost in a clean pot. Dribble compost around the roots and carefully firm it. Support the stem until the plant is established. Do not throw away the old plant. Instead, cut it to about 23cm (9in) high and place in gentle warmth, about 12–18°C (54–64°F). Young shoots will develop from the stem to form a multi-stemmed plant.

Houseplants suitable for air-layering

Dieffenbachia (Dumb Cane)
Ficus elastica (Rubber Plant)
Monstera deliciosa (Swiss Cheese Plant)

PLANTS WITH PLANTLETS

HOUSEPLANTS FROM PLANTLETS

A few houseplants develop small plantlets along or at the edges of leaves; these can be removed and encouraged to produce roots and develop into separate plants.

Step-by-step: plants with plantlets

1. Choose a healthy mother plant (such as this *Kalanchoe daigremontiana*) and gently detach plantlets growing along a leaf's edges.

2. Fill a pot that is 7.5cm (3in) wide with compost and firm it to about 12mm (½in) below the rim. Space out plantlets on the surface and slightly press them into the compost. Gently water the plantlets from above, taking care not to disturb them.

3. When rooted and growing strongly, transfer them to individual small pots. When potting up rooted plantlets of *Kalanchoe delagoensis*, put three plants in each pot.

HOUSEPLANTS FROM RUNNERS

Some houseplants produce plantlets at the ends of long, runner-like stems, perhaps the best known example being *Chlorophytum comosum* (Spider Plant). Although this can be performed throughout the year, late spring to late summer is best.

Step-by-step: increasing a Spider Plant

1. Water the compost in the mother plant and select several long, healthy stems, each with a healthy plantlet at its end. Fill several pots with compost and firm it to 12mm (½in) below the rim. Position a plantlet in the compost and use U-shaped pieces of wire to hold it in place. Lightly water the compost and stand the mother plant and the pots with pegged-down plantlets in a large seedtray. This makes it easy to move them as a unit.

2. When new shoots develop from the plantlet, sever the runner close to the plantlet. Also, cut off the stem close to the mother plant's base.

INCREASING A SPIDER PLANT

Other houseplants with runners and plantlets

Kalanchoe daigremontiana (Mexican Hat)
Kalanchoe delagoensis (Chandelier Plant)
Saxifraga stolonifera (Mother of Thousands)
Saxifraga stolonifera 'Tricolor' (Magic Carpet)

PART TWO
PLANT DIRECTORY

FOLIAGE PLANTS

Foliage houseplants are popular, creating colour and interest over a long period, with only old age or neglect spoiling their display and shortening life expectancy. Many plants, such as variegated ivies and aspidistras, have long been living features in homes. Others are less hardy, but well worth growing.

 HEIGHT   **SPREAD**   **WINTER**   **SUMMER**   **CARE**   **PROPAGATION**

Aglaonema commutatum
Chinese Evergreen
Evergreen perennial with lance-shaped, dark-green leaves up to 13cm (5in) long and 5cm (2in) wide, and having silvery-grey zones on either side of the lateral veins. During midsummer it produces white spathes (arum-type flowers), 5cm (2in) long, followed by dark red berries. There are several forms, including Golden Evergreen (*Aglaonema commutatum* 'Pseudobracteatum', sometimes sold as *Aglaonema pseudobracteatum*), with rich green, spear-shaped leaves and creamy-gold markings.

	15–20cm (6–8in)		10–16°C (50–61°F) Direct light without full sun
	23–30cm (9–12in)		16–24°C (61–75°F) Indirect light

 In winter, keep compost evenly moist; in summer, water more freely and feed every 3–4 weeks. Repot in spring, usually every 3–4 years.

 Divide congested plants when being repotted. Until established, place in 10–16°C (50–61°F).

Anthurium crystallinum
Crystal Anthurium

Evergreen perennial with heart-shaped leaves, up to 60cm (2ft) long and 30cm (1ft) wide. They are violet when young, maturing to deep green, with veins and mid-ribs on the upper surfaces lined in ivory; pale pink beneath.

	38–45cm (15–18in)		13–16°C (55–61°F) Indirect light
	30–38cm (12–15in)		16–21°C (61–70°F) Light shade

 In winter, keep compost barely moist; in summer, water freely but ensure good drainage, and feed every 2–3 weeks with weak liquid fertilizer. Repot in spring when roots fill the pot, usually every 2–3 years.

 Divide congested plants in spring, ensuring each new plant has a growing point. Alternatively, sow seeds in late spring or early summer; place in 24°C (75°F).

Aphelandra squarrosa
Saffron Spike, Zebra Plant

Evergreen shrub with lance-shaped, dark-green leaves, up to 23cm (9in) long, and veins heavily lined in ivory. Yellow, cone-shaped flower heads, 7.5–10cm (3–4in) long, appear from mid- to late summer. 'Louisae' has yellow flowers streaked red and slightly narrower leaves, with bold white markings along the veins. Other forms include 'Brockfeld' (crinkle-edged leaves with ivory lines), 'Dania' (compact, with white veins) and 'Leopoldii' (pale yellow flowers and dark-green leaves with white veins).

	30–60cm (1–2ft)		10–13°C (50–55°F) Full sun or direct light without full sun
	30–38cm (12–15in)		13–18°C (55–64°F) Direct light without full sun

 In winter, keep compost barely moist, and feed at 3-week intervals if the plant is actively growing; in summer, keep it moist but not waterlogged, and feed every 2 weeks. Repot in spring, usually every year.

 Take 7.5–10cm (3–4in) long cuttings during spring and early summer; place in 21°C (70°F).

Asparagus densiflorus 'Myersii'
Foxtail Fern, Plume Asparagus

Sometimes known as *Asparagus densiflorus* 'Meyeri', this fern-like, evergreen perennial initially has an upright nature, then arches, with stiff, spire-like stems packed with bright green, needle-like leaves.

↕ 30–45cm (12–18in)	❄ 10–13°C (50–55°F) Direct light without full sun
↔ 45–75cm (1½–2½ft)	☀ 10–16°C (50–61°F) Indirect light or light shade

In winter, keep compost only slightly moist; water freely in summer, and feed every 2 weeks with weak liquid fertilizer. Repot in spring when roots fill the pot, usually every 1–2 years.

Divide congested plants in spring or early summer. Until established, place in 10–13°C (50–55°F).

Asparagus densiflorus 'Sprengeri'
Asparagus Fern, Emerald Feather, Emerald Fern, Sprengeri Asparagus, Sprenger's Asparagus

Earlier known as *Asparagus sprengeri*, this arching, sprawling, semi-prostrate evergreen perennial has wiry, trailing stems with bright green, needle-like leaves. 'Compactus' is dwarf and less trailing.

↕ 25–30cm (10–12in)	❄ 7–10°C (45–50°F) Direct light without full sun
↔ 75–90cm (2½–3ft), sometimes more	☀ 10–16°C (50–61°F) Indirect light or light shade

In winter, keep compost only slightly moist; water more freely in summer and feed every 2 weeks with weak liquid fertilizer. Repot in spring when roots fill the pot, usually every 1–2 years.

Divide congested plants in spring or early summer. Until established, place in 10°C (50°F).

Asparagus setaceus
Asparagus Fern, Fern Asparagus, Florist Fern, Lace Fern
Earlier known as *Asparagus plumosus,* this evergreen perennial is really a climbing plant, but in its juvenile, non-climbing stage is an ideal houseplant, with mid-green, lace-like leaves borne in horizontal tiers.

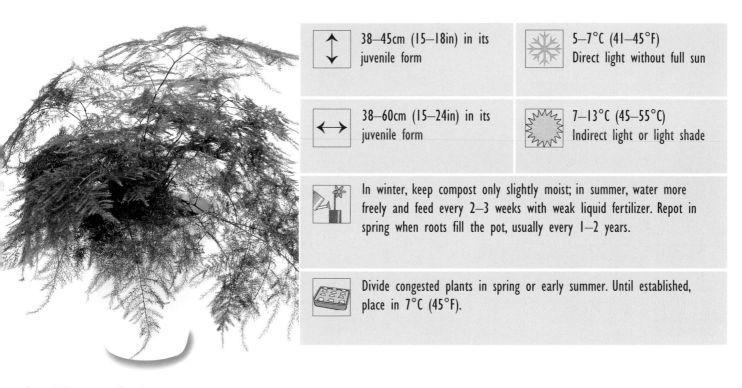

↕ 38–45cm (15–18in) in its juvenile form	❄ 5–7°C (41–45°F) Direct light without full sun
↔ 38–60cm (15–24in) in its juvenile form	☀ 7–13°C (45–55°C) Indirect light or light shade

In winter, keep compost only slightly moist; in summer, water more freely and feed every 2–3 weeks with weak liquid fertilizer. Repot in spring when roots fill the pot, usually every 1–2 years.

Divide congested plants in spring or early summer. Until established, place in 7°C (45°F).

Aspidistra elatior
Barroom Plant, Cast Iron Plant, Iron Plant, Parlour Plant
Earlier known as *Aspidistra lurida,* this evergreen perennial has glossy, dark-green, oblong to lance-shaped leaves, up to 50cm (20in) long. The variegated form (*Aspidistra elatior* 'Variegata') has green leaves striped whitish-cream.

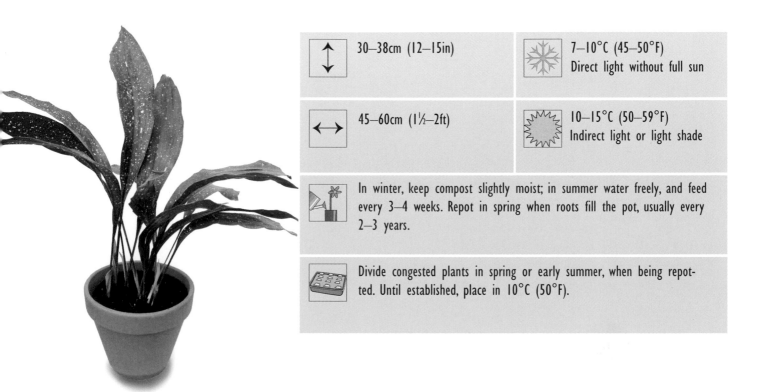

↕ 30–38cm (12–15in)	❄ 7–10°C (45–50°F) Direct light without full sun
↔ 45–60cm (1½–2ft)	☀ 10–15°C (50–59°F) Indirect light or light shade

In winter, keep compost slightly moist; in summer water freely, and feed every 3–4 weeks. Repot in spring when roots fill the pot, usually every 2–3 years.

Divide congested plants in spring or early summer, when being repotted. Until established, place in 10°C (50°F).

Begonia bowerae
Eyelash Begonia

Earlier known as *Begonia boweri*, this small-leaved begonia has irregularly triangular, green leaves that are about 7.5cm (3in) long; they are peppered with chocolate-brown spots. From late winter to late spring, it produces pale pink or white flowers. Begonia 'Tiger' (illustrated below), is a hybrid of *Begonia bowerae* and sometimes sold as *Begonia bowerae 'Tiger'*.

↕	15–25cm (6–10in)	❄	13°C (55°F) Direct light without full sun
↔	15–25cm (6–10in)	☀	13–16°C (55–61°F) Indirect light

In winter, keep compost just moist; in summer, water freely, and feed every 2 weeks. Repot in spring when roots fill the pot, often every year when the plant is young.

Divide congested plants in spring. Until established, place in 13°C (55°F).

Begonia masoniana
Iron Cross Begonia

Rhizomatous-rooted begonia with large, lopsided, slightly heart-shaped green leaves with corrugated surfaces, distinctively patterned with 4–5 deep bronze-purple bars radiating from the centre. It occasionally produces small, greenish-white flowers during spring and summer.

↕	20–25cm (8–10in)	❄	13–15°C (55–59°F) Direct light without full sun
↔	25–30cm (10–12in)	☀	13–20°C (55–68°F) Indirect light

In winter, keep compost barely moist, allowing it to dry slightly between waterings; in summer, water freely without continually saturating the compost, and feed every 2–3 weeks. Repot in spring when roots fill the pot, usually every year when young.

Divide congested plants in spring, when being repotted. Alternatively, take leaf-cuttings in late spring or early summer and place in 13–16°C (55–61°F).

Begonia rex
King Begonia, Painted-leaf Begonia, Rex Begonia

This rhizomatous-rooted perennial has large, slightly heart-shaped, lopsided, wrinkle-surfaced, dark-green leaves with silvery zones near their edges. It is rarely grown: it is mainly the related plants, known as Rex Hybrids, that are seen. The hybrid forms have colourful leaves, up to 25cm (10in) long, that create dominant displays. Many named forms exist.

 23–30cm (9–12in)

 13–15°C (55–59°F) Direct light without full sun

 30–38cm (12–15in)

 13–18°C (55–64°F) Indirect light

 In winter, keep compost barely moist, allowing it to dry slightly between waterings; in summer, water freely without continually saturating the compost, and feed every 2–3 weeks. Repot in spring when roots fill the pot, usually every year when young.

 Divide congested plants in spring, when being repotted, or take leaf-cuttings in late spring or early summer. Cut leaves into squares or triangles and place in 13–16°C (55–61°F).

Calathea makoyana
Brain Plant, Cathedral Plant, Cathedral Windows, Peacock Plant

Earlier known as *Maranta makoyana*, this beautiful evergreen perennial has oval silvery-green leaves, 15cm (6in) long, with mid-green edges irregularly marked by dark-green splashes. The undersides have reddish-purple splashes.

 38–45cm (15–18in)

 13–16°C (55–61°F) Direct light without full sun

 38–45cm (15–18in)

 16–21°C (61–70°F) Indirect light or light shade

 In winter, keep compost evenly moist; in summer water freely, and feed every 2 weeks. Repot in spring when roots fill the pot, usually every year when young.

 Divide congested plants in spring. Until established, place in 13–16°C (55–61°F).

Chlorophytum comosum
Ribbon Plant, Saint Bernard's Lily, Spider Ivy, Spider Plant, Walking Anthericum

Evergreen perennial with long, narrow green leaves striped white. There are several attractive cultivars, including 'Variegatum' (green leaves edged white or cream), 'Vittatum' (central white strip, green edges) and 'Mandanum' (earlier listed as 'Mandaianum', with a central yellow stripe and green edges). Plants develop long, stiff but flexible stems with small plantlets at their ends.

 20–25cm (8–10in), then cascading and trailing

 7–10°C (45–50°F) Direct light without full sun

 38–60cm (15–24in)

 10–18°C (50–64°F) Indirect light, or direct light without full sun

 In winter, keep compost barely moist but not dry; in summer, water freely but ensure good drainage, and feed every 10–14 days. Repot in spring when roots fill the pot – every year when young; later, every other year. When congested, roots swell and push the plant out of the pot, making watering difficult.

 Divide congested plants when being repotted. Also, peg down plantlets into compost. Place in 10–13°C (50–55°F) until established and showing signs of growth.

Cissus antarctica
Kangaroo Vine

Vigorous evergreen perennial climber that develops glossy, heart-shaped and pointed dark-green leaves, about 10cm (4in) long and 5cm (2in) wide, with scalloped and spiny edges.

 1.8–2.4m (6–8ft) when in a pot

 7–10°C (45–50°F) Direct light without full sun

 60–90cm (2–3ft) when in a pot

 10–18°C (50–64°F) Indirect light or light shade

 In winter, keep compost just moist; in summer water freely, and feed every 2–3 weeks. Repot in spring when roots fill the pot, usually every 1–2 years.

 Take 7.5–10cm (3–4in) long cuttings from side-shoots during midsummer and place in 16°C (61°F).

Cissus rhombifolia
Grape Ivy, Natal Vine, Venezuela Treebine

Earlier known as *Rhoicissus rhomboidea*, this will climb and spread to 6m (20ft) in a greenhouse or conservatory. Dark-green leaves are each formed of 3 diamond-shaped, scalloped, spiny-edged leaflets. The form 'Ellen Danica', known as the Mermaid Vine (pictured), is not as vigorous as the species; it is ideal for growing in a pot indoors.

 1.2–1.8m (4–6ft) in a pot indoors

 7–10°C (45–50°F) Full sun

 30–45cm (1–1½ft) in a pot indoors

 10–16°C (50–61°F) Light shade

 In winter, keep compost just moist; in summer, water freely, and feed every 2–3 weeks. Repot in spring when roots fill the pot, usually every 1–2 years.

 Take 7.5–10cm (3–4in) cuttings from side-shoots during midsummer and place in 16°C (61°F).

Codiaeum variegatum var. pictum
Croton, Joseph's Coat, Variegated Laurel

Evergreen perennial with a range of dazzling colours on leathery leaves, which vary in shape and pattern. In greenhouses, these plants reach 2.4–3m (8–10ft) high, but are superb for decorating homes when young and in small pots. The range includes 'Bravo' (green splashed with yellow), 'Carrierei' (yellow-green leaves maturing to reveal red centres), 'Disraeli' (slender mid-green leaves blotched creamy-yellow), 'Holuffiana' (cream veining on forked leaves) and 'Mrs Iceton' (oval, black-green leaves marked between the veins with red and pink).

 45–60cm (1½–2ft) – range

 13–15°C (55–59°F) Full sun, or direct light without full sun

 30–45cm (1–1½ft) – range

 15–18°C (59–64°F) Direct light without full sun

 In winter, keep compost barely moist; in summer, water more freely, but ensure compost is well drained, and feed every 2–3 weeks. Repot in spring when roots fill the pot, usually every year when young.

 Take 7.5cm (3in) cuttings during spring or early summer. Place in 24°C (75°F).

Coleus blumei
Coleus, Flame Nettle, Painted Nettle, Poor Man's Croton

Now known as *Solenostemon scutellarioides,* this popular plant has richly coloured, nettle-like leaves in brilliant shades of red, maroon, yellow and green. They have scalloped or saw-toothed edges. Tubular, blue and white flowers appear during late summer and into autumn, but are best nipped off to prevent them detracting from the beauty of the leaves. There is a wide range of named hybrids, most with a bushy nature, but some trailing. They can be over-wintered in warm rooms or heated greenhouses and conservatories, but are best discarded in early winter and replaced by fresh plants in early summer.

 38–45cm (15–18in)

 13°C (55°F) if over-wintered
Full sun, or direct light without full sun

 30–38cm (12–15in)

 10–15°C (50–59°F)
Full sun, but shade from strong midday sunlight

 In winter, keep over-wintered plants barely moist; in summer, water freely and feed every 2–3 weeks. Repot young plants in spring.

 From mid-spring to late summer take stem-tip cuttings, 7.5–10cm (3–4in) long, and place in 16–18°C (61–64°F). Repot into individual pots when rooted. They can also be raised from seeds.

Cordyline fruticosa
Flaming Dragon, Good Luck Plant, Hawaiian Good Luck Plant, Polynesian Ti, Red Dracaena, Ti Log, Ti Plant, Tree of Kings

Earlier known as *Cordyline terminalis* and *Dracaena terminalis,* this evergreen has lance-shaped, mid- to deep-green leaves flushed with red, purple or cream. Cultivars include 'Guilfoylei' (leaves striped red and pink or white), 'Red Edge' (green, streaked red) and 'Tricolor' (red and purple).

 45–90cm (1½–3ft) in an indoor pot

 10–13°C (50–55°F)
Direct light without full sun

 38–45cm (15–18in) in an indoor pot

 13–24°C (55–75°F)
Direct light without full sun, or light shade

 In winter, keep compost lightly moist; in summer, water more freely and feed every 2 weeks. Repot in spring when roots fill the pot, usually every 2–3 years.

 During midsummer, cut up the stems of old and leggy plants into 7.5cm (3in) pieces. Insert them in equal parts moist peat and sharp sand and place in 18–21°C (64–70°F).

Ctenanthe oppenheimiana
Never-never Plant

Evergreen perennial with a bushy nature and lance-shaped, leathery green leaves with silvery-grey feathering above and purple to wine-red below. Leaves are borne on long stalks. It is usually grown in the form 'Tricolor', with a velvety surface and cream-coloured blotches between leaves and reddish-purple beneath.

 20–30cm (8–12in)

 16°C (61°F)
Direct light without full sun

 25–38cm (10–15in)

 16–21°C (61–70°F)
Direct light without full sun, or indirect light

 In winter, keep compost evenly moist; in summer, water more freely and feed every 2–3 weeks. Repot in spring when roots fill the pot, usually every 2 years

 Divide congested plants in spring and place in 16–18°C (61–64°F) until established.

Dieffenbachia maculata
Dumb Cane, Leopard Lily, Spotted Dog Cane

Also known as *Dieffenbachia picta*, this evergreen perennial has oblong leaves, up to 30cm (12in) long, in various colours. It gains the name Dumb Cane from the sap, which causes loss of speech for a short while after contact with the mouth. Avoid getting sap into your eyes. There are many cultivars, including 'Exotica' (leaves suffused yellow and green) and 'Rudolph Roehrs' (pale yellow, with some veins in ivory).

 45cm–1.2m (1½–4ft)

 15–18°C (59–64°F)
Full sun, or direct light without full sun

 30–45cm (1–1½ft)

 18–24°C (64–75°F)
Indirect light or light shade

 In winter, keep compost evenly but barely moist; in summer, water freely but ensure good drainage, and feed every 2–3 weeks. Repot in spring when roots fill the pot, usually every 2–3 years.

 In spring, cut bare stems into 5–7.5cm (2–3in) pieces, peg them horizontally onto compost and place in 21–24°C (70–75°F).

X *Fatshedera lizei*

Aralia Ivy, Botanical Wonder, Fat-headed Lizzie, Ivy Tree, Miracle Plant, Tree Ivy

Evergreen shrub-like climber with 5-lobed green leaves. When young, it has a single stem, but develops further stems with age, then sprawls and climbs. It can be kept bushy by pinching out the growing tips to encourage further side-shoots to develop. 'Variegata' has leaves with creamy-white blotches and edges, and is less vigorous than the all-green type.

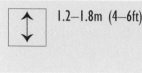 1.2–1.8m (4–6ft)

 4–7°C (39–45°F)
Direct light without full sun, or indirect light

 60–90cm (2–3ft)

 10–18°C (50–64°F); avoid high temperatures
Indirect light or light shade

 In winter, keep compost barely moist, but give more water if the temperature rises; in summer, water freely and feed every 2–3 weeks. Repot in spring when roots fill the pot, usually every year.

 From late spring to midsummer, take 10–13cm (4–5in) cuttings. Place in 16°C (61°F).

Fatsia japonica

False Castor Oil Plant, Formosa Rice Tree, Glossy-leaved Paper Plant, Japanese Fatsia, Paper Plant

Often erroneously known as the Castor Oil Plant (*Ricinus communis*), this moderately hardy, shrub-like plant has large, palm-like, rich glossy-green leaves with 7–9 coarsely tooth-edged lobes. Clusters of rounded white flowers appear only occasionally on houseplants. 'Variegata' has white tips and edges to its leaves.

 90cm–1.5m (3–5ft) indoors or in a conservatory

 3–7°C (37–45°F); avoid high temperatures
Direct light without full sun

 75cm–1.2m (2½–4ft) indoors or in a conservatory

 10–18°C (50–64°F); avoid high temperatures
Indirect to bright light, without full sun

 In winter, keep compost just moist; in summer, water more freely and feed every 2–3 weeks. Repot in spring, usually every year when young.

 When repotting, remove and repot sucker-like shoots from around its base and place in 7–10°C (45–50°F) until rooted.

Ficus benjamina

Benjamin Fig Tree, Benjamin Tree, Java Fig, Small-leaved Rubber Plant, Tropical Laurel, Weeping Fig

Graceful, evergreen shrub or tree with slightly pendulous branches bearing stiff leaves, light green at first, darkening later. There are several superb forms, with narrow or variegated leaves.

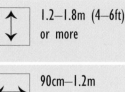 1.2–1.8m (4–6ft) or more

 13–16°C (55–61°F)
Direct light without full sun

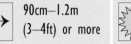 90cm–1.2m (3–4ft) or more

 Avoid excessively high temperatures, i.e. above 24°C (75°F)
Direct light without full sun, or indirect light

 In winter, keep compost lightly moist; in summer, water more freely and feed every 2–3 weeks. Repot in spring when roots fill the pot, usually every 2 years. Top-dress large plants.

 Take 5–10cm (2–4in) cuttings during late spring and early summer. Place in 16–18°C (61–64°F).

Ficus elastica

Assam Rubber, India Rubber Fig, India Rubber Plant, Rambong-rubber, Rubber Plant, Snake Tree

Widely grown houseplant with a single stem and stiff, glossy leaves. There are many forms, including 'Decora' (dark 30cm (1ft) leaves), 'Doescheri' (pink-tinted, pale-green leaves with ivory edges), 'Schrijveriana' (variegated cream patches), 'Tricolor' (cream variegations, sometimes flushed pink) and 'Black Prince' (near-black foliage).

 90cm–1.5m (3–5ft) when young

 16–18°C (61–64°F)
Direct light without full sun

 45–60cm (1½–2ft) when young

 16–24°C (61–75°F)
Indirect light, or direct light without full sun

 In winter, keep compost lightly moist; in summer, water more freely and feed every 2–3 weeks. Repot in spring when roots fill the pot, usually every 2 years. When plants are large, top-dress the compost instead of repotting.

 Take 10–15cm (4–6in) cuttings during late spring and early summer. Place them in 21–24°C (70–75°F). Alternatively, air-layer (see pages 34–35) large plants with bare stems in early and midsummer.

Ficus pumila
Climbing Fig, Climbing Rubber Plant, Creeping Fig, Creeping Rubber Plant

Earlier known as a *Ficus repens*, this evergreen has a climbing, trailing nature and heart-shaped, dark-green leaves. Attractive cultivars include 'Minima' (small leaves, compact), 'Sonny' (variegated leaves with white edges) and 'Variegata' (leaves lined and marbled in cream and green).

↕	1.2–1.5m (4–5ft), more when grown as a climber	❄	7–10°C (45–50°F) Direct light without full sun
↔	1.2–1.5m (4–5ft), more when grown as a climber	☀	10–16°C (50–61°F) Indirect light or light shade

In winter, keep compost lightly moist; in summer, water freely and feed every 2 weeks. Repot in spring when roots fill the pot, usually every 2 years.

Take 5–10cm (2–4in) long cuttings during spring and early summer. Place in 18°C (64°F).

Hedera canariensis 'Gloire de Marengo'
Variegated Canary Island Ivy

Earlier known as *Hedera canariensis* 'Variegata', this hardy, resilient evergreen climber has large, slightly lobed green leaves with dominant silvery-grey centres, merging to white at the edges.

↕	1.5–2.4m (5–8ft) in an indoor pot	❄	2–7°C (35–45°F); avoid high temperatures Direct light without full sun, or indirect light
↔	Climber	☀	7–10°C (45–50°F); avoid high temperatures Indirect light

In winter, keep compost lightly moist; in summer, water freely and feed every 2–3 weeks. Repot in spring when roots fill the pot, usually every 3 years. Top-dress large plants.

Take 7.5–10cm (3–4in) stem- or tip-cuttings in midsummer. Place in 15–18°C (59–64°F).

Hedera helix

Common Ivy, English Ivy

Evergreen climber with a variable nature. Young plants have smaller and more lobed leaves than old ones. The range of cultivars used as houseplants is wide, including all-green types and variegated types (*see* box below).

 45–90cm (1½–3ft) when indoors

 Climbing and trailing

 5–10°C (41–50°F) Full sun, or direct light without full sun

 10–16°C (50–61°F) Indirect light or light shade

 In winter, keep compost lightly moist; in summer, water more freely, and feed every 2–3 weeks. Repot in spring when roots fill the pot, usually every 3 years. Top-dress large plants.

 Take 7.5cm (3in) stem-cuttings in summer. Place in 15–18°C (59–64°F).

Hedera helix cultivars

Small, all-green leaves	Variegated leaves
'Annette' (also known as 'California'): matt-green, 5-lobed leaves	**'Eva'** leaves variegated cream and green
'Chicago' 5-lobed leaves	**'Glacier'** long a popular houseplant ivy; 3 distinctive lobes variegated silvery-grey, with creamy-white edges
'Green Ripple' usually 3-lobed leaves with distinctive and attractive veins	**'Harald'** leaves variegated two-tone green and cream
'Parsley Crested' (often sold as *Hedera helix cristata* and widely known as Parsley Ivy): 5-lobed leaves with wavy-edges	**'Jubilee'** dark-green leaves with golden centres
'Pittsburgh' robust nature, 5-lobed leaves	**'Kolibri'** leaves variegated green and white

Hypoestes phyllostachya
Baby's Tears, Dot Plant, Flamingo Plant, Freckle Face, Measles Plant, Pink Dot, Pink Polka, Polka Dot Plant
Earlier known as *Hypoestes sanguinolenta,* this bushy, sprawling, evergreen perennial produces a mass of oval, olive-green, spear-tipped leaves covered with white to pinkish spots and blotches. Superb cultivars include 'Bettina' (lighter-coloured markings), 'Carmina' (bright red leaves), 'Purpuriana' (plum-coloured markings) and 'Wit' (leaves marbled white).

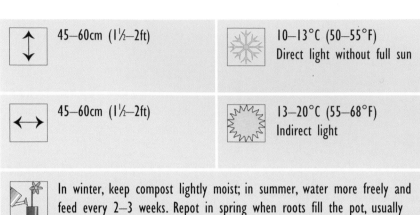

↕	45–60cm (1½–2ft)
↔	45–60cm (1½–2ft)
❄	10–13°C (50–55°F) Direct light without full sun
☀	13–20°C (55–68°F) Indirect light

 In winter, keep compost lightly moist; in summer, water more freely and feed every 2–3 weeks. Repot in spring when roots fill the pot, usually every year when young.

Take 7.5cm (3in) tip-cuttings in late spring and early summer. Place in 21°C (70°F).

Maranta leuconeura
Prayer Plant, Ten Commandments
Evergreen perennial with beautiful leaves that close in the evening and are held erect, as if in prayer. Young leaves have an emerald-green background, with brown-purple blotches between the veins. The undersides are grey-green, shot with purple. There are several forms, including *Maranta leuconeura* 'Kerchoveana' (*Maranta kerchoveana*), widely known as Rabbit's Tracts or Rabbit's Foot (descriptive of the leaves). At first, the leaves are emerald-green with red blotches between the main veins, but with age become dark-green with maroon blotches. *Maranta leuconeura* 'Erythrophylla' (Herringbone Plant) – also known as *Maranta leuconeura tricolor, Maranta erythrophylla* and *Maranta leuconera* 'Erthyroneura' – has leaves with a deep olive-green background, greyish-green edges, vivid red veins and bright green, irregular-edged markings along the mid-rib.

↕	15–20cm (6–8in)
↔	25–30cm (10–12in)
❄	13–16°C (55–61°F) Direct light without full sun
☀	16–18°C (61–64°F) Indirect light or light shade

 In winter, keep compost lightly moist; in summer, water more freely and feed every 2–3 weeks. Repot in spring when roots fill the pot, usually every year when young.

 Divide congested plants when being repotted and place in 16°C (61°F) until established.

Monstera deliciosa

Breadfruit Vine, Ceriman, Cheese Plant, Cut-leaf Philodendron, Fruit Salad Plant, Hurricane Plant, Mexican Breadfruit, Monstera, Split-leaf Philodendron, Swiss Cheese Plant, Window Plant

Evergreen perennial with a climbing, sprawling nature. Dark-green leaves can be 1m (3½ft) long and 45–60cm (1½–2ft) wide. Indoors, leaves are smaller, deeply notched and perforated. Mature plants have creamy-yellow spathes up to 15cm (6in) long, followed by club-shaped fruits. 'Variegata' has marbled leaves streaked with cream and yellow.

 1.8–3.6m (6–12ft), sometimes more

 7–10°C (45–50°C) Full sun

 90cm–1.5m (3–5ft)

 10–21°C (50–70°C) Direct light without full sun, or indirect light

 In winter, keep compost moist; in summer, water more freely, but allow to become slightly dry between waterings. Feed every 2–3 weeks in summer, avoiding strong concentrations, which damage roots. Repot in spring when roots fill the pot, usually every year when young. Later, just top-dress the compost.

 During early summer, cut off the growing tip, together with a mature leaf and an aerial root, if possible. Insert the cutting in equal parts moist peat and sharp sand and place in 24–27°C (75–80°F).

Ophiopogon jaburan

Jaburan Lily, Jaburan Lilyturf, Snakebeard, White Lily, White Lilytuft

Evergreen perennial with stiff, but arching, narrow grass-like, all-green leaves. Variegated forms are more usually grown, including 'Vittatus' (sometimes known as 'Variegatus'), 'Argenteo-vittatus' and 'Aureo-variegatus', all with yellow- or white-striped leaves.

 25–38cm (10–15in)

 5–10°C (41–50°F) Direct light without full sun, or full sun

 25–38cm (10–15in)

 10–16°C (50–61°F) Direct light without full sun

 In winter, keep compost evenly moist; in summer, water more freely and feed every 2–3 weeks. Repot in spring when roots fill the pot, often every year.

 Divide congested plants when being repotted and place in 10°C (50°F) until established.

PELARGONIUM

A group of popular houseplants with a sub-shrubby nature, Pelargoniums are often confusingly called geraniums because their leaf shapes resemble those of the garden geranium (a herbaceous perennial totally unrelated to pelargoniums). Several types of pelargoniums are used to decorate homes, some with superb flowers, others with attractive leaves. On the opposite page are some with scented leaves.

See individual plants on page 55

See individual plants on page 55

In temperate climates plants can be overwintered in a greenhouse or conservatory in 7–10°C (45–50°F)
Direct light

13–16°C (55–61°F)
Direct light, but provide light shade if the temperature rises dramatically

In winter, keep compost barely moist, but water more freely in summer.

Take stem-tip cuttings, about 7.5cm (3in) long, in mid- and late summer. Insert in equal parts moist peat and sharp sand. Place in 13–16°C (55–61°F) on a greenhouse bench and cover initially with a couple of sheets of newspaper. When rooted, transfer the cuttings to individual pots.

Pelargonium capitatum
Rose Geranium, Rose-scented Geranium
Soft-stemmed plant with light-green, deeply lobed, velvety, somewhat crinkled leaves with a rose-like fragrance. It produces mauve-pink flowers with darker veins.

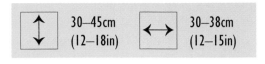

Pelargonium crispum
Lemon Geranium, Lemon-scented Geranium
Slender shrub, with green, hoary, deeply lobed leaves with a distinctive lemon and balm fragrance when bruised. Rose-pink flowers appear in umbrella-like heads from early to late summer. Closely related *Pelargonium crispum* 'Minor' (Finger Bowl Pelargonium) has leaves with a sweet and citron-like fragrance.

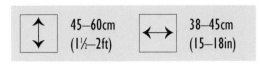

Pelargonium x fragrans
Nutmeg Geranium
Soft-stemmed shrub with grey-green, velvety, 3-lobed leaves with a nutmeg and pine redolence. The flowers are white and prominently spotted and veined in red.

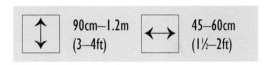

Pelargonium graveolens
Rose Geranium, Rose-scented Geranium, Sweet-scented Geranium
Hoary, green, deeply lobed leaves reveal a sweet, rose-like fragrance when bruised. It produces rose-pink flowers with dark purple spots during mid- and late summer.

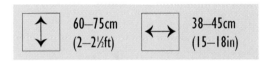

Pelargonium odoratissimum
Apple-scented Geranium
Somewhat sprawling plant with light-green, velvety, round to heart-shaped leaves with a ripe-apple scent. Small, white flowers in summer.

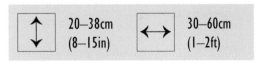

Pelargonium quercifolium
Almond-scented Geranium, Almond-scented Pelargonium, Oak-leaved Geranium, Village Oak Geranium
Triangular to oblong, lobed and tooth-edged, mid-green leaves with the fragrance of almond combined with a hint of balsam. It has rose-coloured flowers with deep purple veins during early and midsummer.

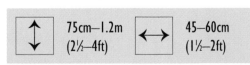

Pelargonium tomentosum
Herb-scented Geranium, Mint Geranium, Peppermint Geranium
Pale-green, soft, hairy leaves with dense, white downy-haired undersides and a distinctive, strong peppermint fragrance. White flowers peppered with red appear during summer.

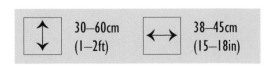

Peperomia caperata
Emerald Ripple, Emerald-ripple Peperomia, Green-ripple Peperomia, Little Fantasy Peperomia

Evergreen perennial with heart-shaped, glistening green leaves with a ripple-like surface. From spring to late autumn it bears white flowers in spikes up to 15cm (6in) high. Occasionally, they branch and have an antler-like nature.

 10–20cm (4–8in) plus height of flowers

 10–13°C (50–55°F) Direct light without full sun

 13–15cm (5–6in)

 13–18°C (55–64°F) Indirect light

 In winter, keep compost barely moist; in summer, water thoroughly, allowing to dry slightly between waterings, and feed every 3–4 weeks. Repot in late spring, when roots fill the pot, usually every 2 years.

 Take leaf-petiole (leaf and leaf-stalk) cuttings during summer. Place in 18°C (64°F).

Philodendron bipinnatifidum
Tree Philodendron

Evergreen perennial with glossy green leaves. Young leaves are heart-shaped; mature ones – up to 60cm (2ft) long and 45cm (1½ft) wide – are broadly 3-lobed and slowly develop deep incisions that may extend almost to the mid-rib.

 90cm–1.2m (3–4ft)

 13–18°C (55–64°F); it can survive temperatures down to 10°C (50°F) for short periods Direct light without full sun

 90cm–1m (3–3½ft)

 18–24°C (64–75°F) Direct light without full sun, or indirect light

 In winter, keep compost just moist; in summer, water more freely, but ensure good drainage (continually wet compost damages roots). Feed every 3 weeks during summer. Repot in spring when roots fill the pot, usually every year when young. Later, top-dress compost, but avoid damaging surface roots.

 Divide congested plants in early summer. Until established, place in 16–18°C (61–64°F).

Philodendron erubescens
Blushing Philodendron, Red-leaf Philodendron

Vigorous evergreen climber with arrow-shaped leaves up to 30cm (12in) long and 18cm (7in) wide on mature plants, borne on long purple leaf-stalks. When young, leaves are rose-pink, slowly becoming dark, glossy green, with a coppery tinge. There are several forms, including 'Red Emerald' (compact, with arrow-shaped leaves, pale bronze when young, becoming dark olive-green with narrow, purplish edges) and 'Burgundy' (young foliage coppery-red, gradually becoming olive-green with burgundy undersides).

 1.2–1.8m (4–6ft)

 13–18°C (55–64°F)
Direct light without full sun

 38–45cm (15–18in)

 18–24°C (64–75°F)
Direct light without full sun, or indirect light

 In winter, keep compost barely moist; in summer, water freely but ensure good drainage, and feed every 3–4 weeks. Repot young plants annually in spring, and thereafter about every 2 years. When large, top-dress the compost. Provide a moss-covered pole for support.

 Divide congested plants in early summer. Place in 16–18°C (61–64°F) until established.

Philodendron scandens
Heartleaf Philodendron, Sweetheart Plant, Sweetheart Vine

Moderately vigorous climbing evergreen perennial that forms a dense array of heart-shaped, mid-green leaves up to 10cm (4in) long and 7.5cm (3in) wide. When young, the leaves have an attractive bronze shade. The variegated form has cream blotches on the lower half of each leaf.

 1–1.5m (3½–5ft)

 13–18°C (55–64°F)
Direct light without full sun

 20–38cm (8–15in)

 18–24°C (64–75°F)
Direct light without full sun, or indirect light

 In winter, keep compost barely moist; in summer, water more freely and feed every 3 weeks. Repot in spring when roots fill the pot, usually every 2 years. Provide a moss-covered pole for support.

 Take 10cm (4in) cuttings in early summer. Place in 21–24°C (70–75°F).

Pilea cadierei
Aluminium Plant, Watermelon Pilea

Evergreen perennial with leathery, oval, dark-green, slightly quilted leaves that have silvery splashes between the veins. The form 'Nana' is smaller, up to 23cm (9in) high. *Pilea* 'Bronze' is similar, with dull bronze-green leaves, 7.5cm (3in) long, and silvery marks between the veins.

 25–30cm (10–12in)

 10–13°C (50–55°F) Direct light without full sun, or indirect light

 20–25cm (8–10in)

 16–24°C (61–75°F) Indirect light

 In winter, keep compost barely moist; in summer, water more freely and feed every 2 weeks. Repot in spring when roots fill the pot, usually every year when young.

 Take 7.5–10cm (3–4in) stem-tip cuttings in spring or early summer. Place in 18–21°C (64–70°F).

Pilea involucrata 'Norfolk'
Friendship Plant, Panamica Panamiga, Pan-American Friendship Plant

This bushy, slightly trailing evergreen perennial has oval to pear-shaped, silvery-grey leaves with bronze-green along the veins. If the plant is in shade, leaves are more green than bronze. The undersides are red.

 20–25cm (8–10in)

 13–16°C (55–61°F) Indirect light or light shade

 20–25cm (8–10in)

 16–24°C (61–75°F) Light shade

 In winter, keep the compost barely moist; in summer, water more freely and feed every 2 weeks. Repot in spring when roots fill the pot, usually every year when young.

 Take 7.5cm (3in) stem-tip cuttings in spring and early summer. Place in 18–21°C (64–70°F).

Pilea microphylla
Artillery Plant, Gunpowder Plant, Mossy Pilea

Earlier known as *Pilea muscosa*, this evergreen perennial with small, mid-green leaves has a fern-like appearance. From late spring to late summer it produces small, greenish-yellow flowers that puff out clouds of pollen when disturbed, causing great amusement, especially to children.

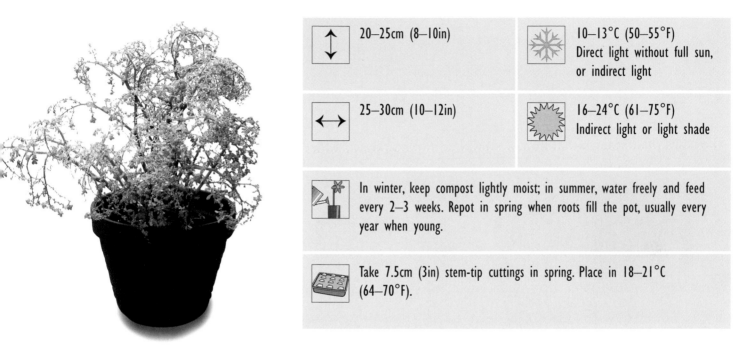

↕ 20–25cm (8–10in)	❄ 10–13°C (50–55°F) Direct light without full sun, or indirect light
↔ 25–30cm (10–12in)	☀ 16–24°C (61–75°F) Indirect light or light shade

In winter, keep compost lightly moist; in summer, water freely and feed every 2–3 weeks. Repot in spring when roots fill the pot, usually every year when young.

Take 7.5cm (3in) stem-tip cuttings in spring. Place in 18–21°C (64–70°F).

Pilea mollis
Moon Valley Plant

Also known as *Pilea* 'Moon Valley' and *Pilea involucrata* 'Moon Valley', this small, bushy perennial has wrinkle-surfaced oval- to pear-shaped, pointed leaves. They are yellowish-green, covered with minute white hairs, contrasted by darker green veining. When young and unfurling, they are almost entirely maroon, with emerald-green edges.

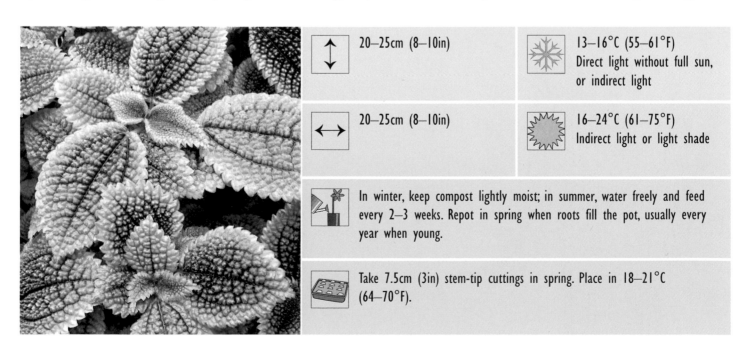

↕ 20–25cm (8–10in)	❄ 13–16°C (55–61°F) Direct light without full sun, or indirect light
↔ 20–25cm (8–10in)	☀ 16–24°C (61–75°F) Indirect light or light shade

In winter, keep compost lightly moist; in summer, water freely and feed every 2–3 weeks. Repot in spring when roots fill the pot, usually every year when young.

Take 7.5cm (3in) stem-tip cuttings in spring. Place in 18–21°C (64–70°F).

Plectranthus coleoides 'Marginatus'
White-edged Candle Plant, White-edged Swedish Ivy

Also known as *Plectranthus forsteri* 'Marginatus', this evergreen perennial produces scalloped-edged, heart-shaped, hairy-surfaced, pale-green leaves with irregular white edges. Each leaf is 5–7.5cm (2–3in) wide.

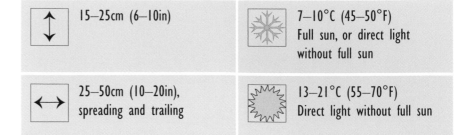

↕ 15–25cm (6–10in)	❄	7–10°C (45–50°F) Full sun, or direct light without full sun
↔ 25–50cm (10–20in), spreading and trailing	☀	13–21°C (55–70°F) Direct light without full sun

 In winter, keep compost just moist; in summer, water freely and feed every 2 weeks. Repot in spring when roots fill the pot, usually every 2–3 years.

 Take 7.5–10cm (3–4in) stem-tip cuttings during spring. Place them in 16–18°C (61–64°F).

Rhoeo spathacea
Boat Lily, Men in a Boat, Moses in his Cradle, Moses in the Bulrushes, Moses on a Raft, Oyster Plant, Purple-leaved Spiderwort, Two Men in a Boat, Three Men in a Boat

Also known as *Tradescantia spathacea*, this evergreen perennial has stiff, lance-shaped, glossy dark-green leaves with rich purple undersides. 'Vittata' (sometimes sold as 'Vittatum' or 'Variegata') has leaves finely striped in cream.

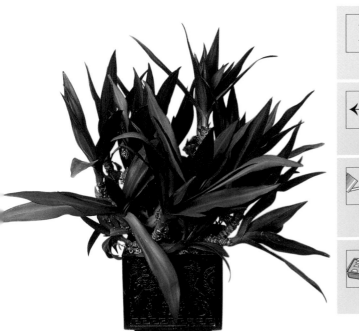

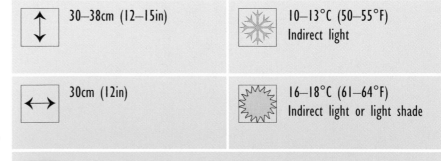

↕ 30–38cm (12–15in)	❄	10–13°C (50–55°F) Indirect light
↔ 30cm (12in)	☀	16–18°C (61–64°F) Indirect light or light shade

 In winter, keep compost evenly moist; in summer, water freely and feed every 2–3 weeks. Repot in spring when roots fill the pot, usually every year when young.

 Take 7.5–10cm (3–4in) long basal shoots in spring. Place them in 16–18°C (61–64°F).

Sansevieria trifasciata
Bowstring Hemp, Devil's Tongue, Good Luck Plant, Mother-in-law's Tongue, Snake Plant

This evergreen succulent has upright, sword-like leaves. *Sansevieria trifasciata* has dark-green leaves with mottled grey transverse bands. *Sansevieria trifasciata* var. *laurentii* is more impressive, with bold, creamy-yellow edges to the leaves. *Sansevieria trifasciata* 'Hahnii' (often sold as *Sansevieria hahnii*) is about 15cm (6in) high, with dark-green leaves that develop transverse grey and yellow bands. 'Golden Hahnii' has yellow edges to its leaves.

 38–45cm (15–18in)

 7–10°C (45–50°F)
Full sun

 15–20cm (6–8in)

 10–21°C (50–70°F)
Full sun

 In winter, keep compost barely moist; in summer, water thoroughly but allow to become slightly dry between applications, and feed every 2 weeks. Repot in spring, but only when the plant totally fills its pot with roots and stems, usually every 2–3 years.

 All can be increased by dividing congested plants when being repotted, but those plants without yellow edges, such as *Sansevieria trifasciata*, can be also be increased by taking leaf-cuttings during summer and placing them in 21°C (70°F).

Saxifraga stolonifera
Beefsteak Geranium, Creeping Sailor, Mother of Thousands, Pedlar's Basket, Rowing Sailor, Strawberry Begonia, Strawberry Geranium

Earlier known as *Saxifraga sarmentosa*, this tufted, trailing evergreen perennial has mid-green, round leaves with silvery veins. Their undersides are flushed red. Long, trailing, wiry stems bear plantlets at their tips, and white flowers appear during summer. 'Tricolor' has leaves variegated white, pink and green, with red edges.

 20–25cm (8–10in)

 5–10°C (41–50°F)
Direct light without full sun

 25–38cm (10–15in) and trailing

 10–18°C (50–64°F)
Indirect light

 In winter, keep compost barely moist; in summer, water freely but ensure good drainage, and feed every 3–4 weeks. Repot in spring when roots fill the pot, usually every year for young and strongly growing plants.

 Peg the plantlets into compost in late spring and summer, and place in 10–18°C (50–64°F).

Schefflera actinophylla

Australian Ivy Palm, Australian Umbrella Tree, Octopus Tree, Queensland Umbrella Tree, Rubber Tree, Star Leaf, Umbrella Plant, Umbrella Tree

Earlier known as *Brassaia actinophylla*, this evergreen tree has leaves formed of leathery, glossy leaflets. Young plants have 3 leaflets to each leaf, more mature plants develop 5 or 7, each about 18cm (7in) long and 5cm (2in) wide.

 1.8–2.4m (6–8ft), sometimes more

 10–13°C (50–55°F) Direct light without full sun

 60–90cm (2–3ft), sometimes more

 13–24°C (55–75°F) Indirect light

 In winter, keep compost moderately moist; in summer, water more freely and feed every 3–4 weeks. Repot in spring when roots fill the pot, usually every 2–3 years. For large plants, top-dress the compost.

 Sow seeds in late winter or early spring in seed-trays. Place in 21–24°C (70–75°F).

Schefflera arboricola

Green Rays, Parasol Plant, Star Leaf, Umbrella Tree

Earlier known as *Heptapleurum arboricolum*, this bushy evergreen has shiny green leaves formed of 7–11 slender leaflets borne like the spokes of a parasol at the tops of stiff stems. 'Variegata' has leaves splashed in yellow.

 1.5–1.8m (5–6ft)

 13–15°C (55–59°F) Direct light without full sun

 45–75cm (1½–2½ft)

 18–24°C (64–75°F) Indirect light

 In winter, keep compost moderately moist; in summer, water freely but ensure good drainage, and feed every 3–4 weeks. Repot in spring when roots fill the pot, usually every 2–3 years. For large plants, top-dress the compost.

 Sow seeds in late winter or early spring in seed-trays. Place in 21–24°C (70–75°F).

Tolmiea menziesii

Pick-a-back Plant, Pig-a-back Plant, Piggy-back Plant, Thousand Mothers, Youth-on-Age

Evergreen perennial with large, hairy, maple-like, mid-green leaves. Small plantlets grow where leaf-stalks join mature leaves. During summer it produces red-flushed, greenish-white flowers on long stems. There are several variegated forms, including 'Taff's Gold'.

 15–20cm (6–8in)

 4–7°C (39–45°F)
Direct light without full sun

 30–38cm (12–15in)

 10–18°C (50–64°F)
Indirect light or light shade

 In winter, keep compost evenly moist; in summer, water more freely and feed every 3 weeks. Repot in spring when roots fill the pot, usually every 1–2 years.

 Divide congested plants in spring. Alternatively, in late spring or summer, sever mature leaves with plantlets attached to them and peg them on the compost surface. When plantlets have developed roots, transfer them to individual pots and place in 7–10°C (45–50°F) until established; later place in 10–18°C (50–64°F).

Tradescantia fluminensis

Inch Plant, Green Wandering Jew, Wandering Jew, Wandering Sailor, White-flowered Spiderwort

Earlier known as *Tradescantia albiflora*, this evergreen perennial has trailing stems with oval green leaves that are 5–7.5cm (2–3in) long, stalkless and appear to partially clasp the stem. Invariably, variegated forms are grown, including 'Albovittata' (leaves striped white), 'Aurea' (yellow with green stripes), and 'Tricolor Minima' (small leaves striped pink, white and mauve).

 10–15cm (4–6in)

 7–10°C (45–50°F)
Direct light without full sun

 Trailing

 10–18°C (50–64°F); avoid high temperatures
Indirect light

 In winter, keep compost barely moist; in summer, water more freely and feed every 2–3 weeks. Repot in spring when roots fill the pot, usually every year when young.

 Take 5–7.5cm (2–3in) stem-tip cuttings in summer. Place in 16°C (61°F).

Tradescantia zebrina
Inch Plant, Silvery Inch Plant, Wandering Jew

Also known as *Tradescantia pendula* and *Zebrina pendula,* this evergreen perennial has green leaves, 5–6.5cm (2–2½in) long, banded in glistening silver, with purple undersides. There are several forms, including 'Quadricolor' (leaves striped green, pink, red and white) and 'Purpusii' (earlier known as *Zebrina purpusii* or *Zebrina pendula purpusii*), with leaves tinged purple.

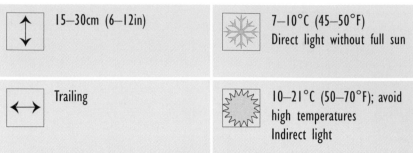

↕ 15–30cm (6–12in)	❄ 7–10°C (45–50°F) Direct light without full sun
↔ Trailing	☀ 10–21°C (50–70°F); avoid high temperatures Indirect light

In winter, keep compost just moist; in summer, water more freely and feed every 2–3 weeks. Repot in spring when roots fill the pot, usually every 1–2 years.

Take 7.5cm (3in) stem-tip cuttings during summer. Place in 16–18°C (61–64°F).

Yucca elephantipes
Izote, Palm Lily, Spineless Yucca

Earlier known as *Yucca guatemalensis*, this tree-like evergreen develops stiff, green leaves up to 90cm (3ft) long, with rough edges. Old plants produce clusters of leaves at their tops, which has encouraged the common name, Palm Lily. Several other yuccas can be grown indoors, including *Yucca aloifolia* (Spanish Bayonet) with stiff, sword-like leaves.

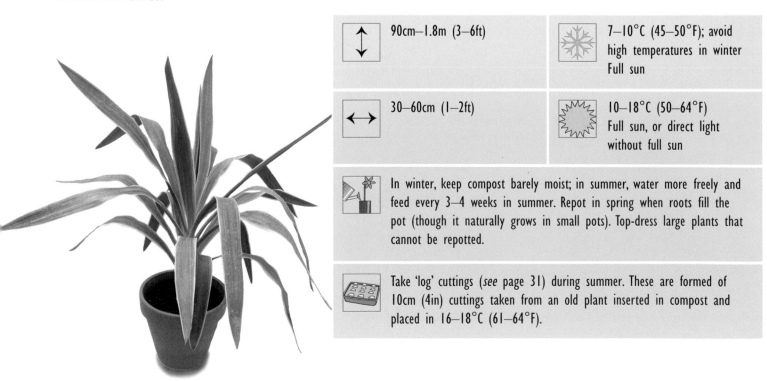

↕ 90cm–1.8m (3–6ft)	❄ 7–10°C (45–50°F); avoid high temperatures in winter Full sun
↔ 30–60cm (1–2ft)	☀ 10–18°C (50–64°F) Full sun, or direct light without full sun

In winter, keep compost barely moist; in summer, water more freely and feed every 3–4 weeks in summer. Repot in spring when roots fill the pot (though it naturally grows in small pots). Top-dress large plants that cannot be repotted.

Take 'log' cuttings (*see* page 31) during summer. These are formed of 10cm (4in) cuttings taken from an old plant inserted in compost and placed in 16–18°C (61–64°F).

OTHER FOLIAGE HOUSEPLANTS

Aglaonema crispum (Painted Drop Tongue): this bushy, evergreen perennial has narrowly oval leaves, mostly silver, with greenish-grey parts.

Begonia metallica (Metallic-leaf Begonia): fibrous roots, lop-sided, triangular-shaped, metallic-green leaves and distinctive purple veins.

Calathea lancifolia (Rattlesnake Plant): long, narrow leaves with crinkly edges and yellowish background. Dark green bands radiate from the midrib.

Calathea zebrina (Zebra Plant): leaves are emerald-green with horizontal dark-green stripes radiating from mid-rib. Purple undersides.

Cordyline australis (Cabbage Tree, Fountain Grass, Giant Dracaena, Giant Fountain Grass, Grass Palm, Grass Plant, Palm Lily): earlier known as *Dracaena australis*, this evergreen perennial grows 7.5m (25ft) or more in the wild, but when young is an ideal houseplant. When young, it has a short stem with arching leaves. Some forms have coloured or striped leaves.

Cyperus alternifolius (Umbrella Grass, Umbrella Plant): upright, stiff stems bear umbrella-like heads of slender, green, leaf-like shoots.

Dracaena deremensis (Dragon Tree): narrow, ribbon-like, stiff, glossy-green leaves. Several variegated forms.

Dracaena godseffiana (Gold Dust Dracaena, Spotted Dracaena): also known as *Dracaena surculosa*, this woody shrub has a lax array of dark-green leaves spotted and splashed with cream.

Epipremnum aureum (Devil's Ivy, Pothos Vine): sometimes sold as *Scindapsus aureus*, its oval and pointed bright green leaves are splashed and streaked in yellow. Several attractive forms.

Episcia cupreata (Flame Violet): large, oval, soft and copper-coloured leaves with silvery veins; orange flowers in summer.

Ficus deltoidea (Mistletoe Fig, Mistletoe Rubber Plant, Mistletree): also known as *Ficus diversifolia*, this slow-growing evergreen shrub or small tree has leathery, dark-green, pear-shaped to oval leaves.

Fittonia verschaffeltii (Painted Net Leaf, Mosaic Plant): somewhat sprawling plant with dark-green leaves distinctively veined in carmine. Several attractive forms.

Grevillea robusta (Silky Oak): deep-green, fern-like leaves covered with silky hairs.

Gynura procumbens (Velvet Plant, Purple Passion Plant): twining and climbing plant with leaves covered with fine, purplish-hairs.

Iresine herbstii (Beef Plant, Beef Steak, Bloodleaf): evergreen perennial with a bushy nature and soft red stems that bear wine-red, heart-shaped leaves about 7.5cm (3in) long with paler red veining.

Pandanus sandieri: perennial evergreen with stiff, arching, long and narrow, mid-green leaves that make it look stemless. Leaves are striped with thin, golden-yellow bands and have spiny edges.

Pandanus veitchii (Screw Pine, Veitch Screw Pine): evergreen perennial with narrow, spine-edged leaves that arch towards their tips. Initially forms a stemless rosette, but later has a stem. The dark-green leaves are striped and edged with white or creamy-white flowers.

Peperomia argyreia (Rugby Football Plant, Silvered Peperomia, Watermelon Begonia): evergreen perennial with oval leaves that taper to a point. The smooth-surfaced leaves are a waxy, bluish-green with silver bands that radiate outwards. Leaf-stalks are usually red.

Peperomia magnoliifolia (Desert Privet): evergreen perennial with a bushy nature and large, fleshy, green leaves. Best grown in one of its variegated forms, such as 'Variegata' (cream variegations) or 'Green and Gold' (cream edges to light-green leaves).

Pilea nummulariifolia (Creeping Charlie): evergreen perennial with a creeping, branching nature. Red, wiry stems branch and bear dark-green, rounded to heart-shaped leaves, with quilted surfaces. They are about 12mm (½in) wide.

FLOWERING HOUSEPLANTS

Flowering houseplants are more permanent features indoors than flowering potplants, which have an ephemeral nature (see pages 79–92). When they are not flowering, they can be placed in a conservatory or heated greenhouse, depending on the time of year.

 HEIGHT   **SPREAD**   **WINTER**   **SUMMER**   **CARE**    **PROPAGATION**

Acalypha hispida
Chenille Plant, Foxtail, Philippine Medusa, Red Cattail, Red-hot Cat's Tail

Earlier known as *Acalypha sanderi*, this woody shrub eventually needs a greenhouse border or large pot in a conservatory, but is an ideal houseplant when young. It produces bright scarlet flowers in long, pendulous tassels in summer and into autumn. One of the forms is shown below.

 90cm–1.2m (3–4ft), up to 2.4m (8ft) or more in a greenhouse border

 15–18°C (59–64°F)
Full sun

 45–75cm (1½–2½ft), up to 1.5m (5ft) or more in a greenhouse border

 16–24°C (61–75°F)
Bright light without full sun

 During winter, keep the compost slightly moist, but water freely in summer. Feed every 2 weeks from late spring to late summer. Repot in late winter or early spring when roots fill the pot, usually every 2–3 years.

 Take 10–13cm (4–5in) stem-tip cuttings in late spring or early summer and insert in equal parts moist peat and sharp sand. Place in 16–24°C (61–75°F).

Aeschynanthus radicans
Basket Vine, Lipstick Plant, Lipstick Vine

Lax, sprawling climber with small, oval, fleshy, dark-green leaves and tubular, hooded, bright red flowers with cream-yellow throats during midsummer.

 45–60cm (1½–2ft)

 13–15°C (55–59°F)
Full sun

 45–60cm (1½–2ft) – trailing

 15–24°C (59–75°F)
Full sun, or direct light without full sun

 During winter, keep compost barely moist; in summer, water freely. From late spring to late summer feed every 4 weeks. Repot in spring when roots fill the pot, usually every 3 years.

 Take 7.5cm (3in) stem-tip cuttings during midsummer and insert in equal parts moist peat and sharp sand. Place in 18–21°C (64–70°F).

Anthurium scherzerianum
Flaming Flower, Flamingo Flower, Flamingo Plant, Pigtail Flower, Pigtail Plant, Tail Flower

It has dark-green, heart-shaped leaves. Palette-shaped, brilliant scarlet spathes, 7.5–10cm (3–4in) long, appear throughout summer, with spiral, orange-red spadices (fleshy, stiff, usually brightly coloured flower spikes).

 23–30cm (9–12in)

 10–13°C (50–55°F)
Indirect light

 30–38cm (12–15in)

 13–24°C (55–75°F)
Light shade

 In winter, keep compost barely moist but not dry; in summer, water freely but ensure good drainage. From late spring to late summer feed every 2–3 weeks. Repot in spring when roots fill the pot, usually every 2–3 years.

 Divide congested plants in spring. Place initially in 10–13°C (50–55°F).

Bougainvillea x buttiana 'Mrs Butt'
Paper Flower

Deciduous climber with a vigorous nature. The flowers are insignificant; it is grown for its cascades of rose-crimson bracts that fade to magenta. There are many cultivars, with papery bracts lasting several months.

 1.5–2.4m (5–8ft) when grown in a large pot (more in border soil in a greenhouse)

 7–10°C (45–50°F) Full sun

 Climber

 10–21°C (50–70°F) Full sun, or direct light without full sun

 In winter, keep compost slightly moist; in summer, water generously but ensure good drainage. From late spring to late summer, feed every 2–3 weeks. Repot in late winter or early spring when roots fill the pot, usually every year when young.

 Take 7.5cm (3in) stem-cuttings with heels (pieces of older wood attached to the cutting's base) during summer. Insert in equal parts moist peat and sharp sand. Place in 21°C (70°F).

Columnea x banksii
Goldfish Plant

Evergreen hybrid clothed in glossy, dark-green leaves. Orange-red flowers, about 7.5cm (3in) long, with orange markings in their throats, appear from early winter to mid-spring.

 Long, trailing stems

 13–16°C (55–61°F) Direct light without full sun

 Trailer

 16–21°C (61–70°F) Indirect light

 In winter, keep compost moist, especially when flowering; in summer, water freely but ensure good drainage. From late spring to late summer feed every 2–3 weeks. Repot in spring when roots fill the pot, usually every other year.

 Take 7.5–10cm (3–4in) long cuttings from non-flowering shoots during spring and early summer and insert in equal parts moist peat and sharp sand. Place in 18–21°C (64–70°F).

Cuphea ignea
Cigar Flower, Cigar Plant, Firecracker Plant, Mexican Cigar Flower, Red-white-and-blue Flower

This short-lived evergreen has smooth-surfaced, lance-shaped, mid-green leaves. Masses of tubular, bright scarlet flowers, 25mm (1in) long, appear from late spring to early winter.

 30–38cm (12–15in), sometimes slightly more

 7–10°C (45–50°F) Full sun, or direct light without full sun

 30–38cm (12–15in), sometimes slightly more

 10–18°C (50–64°F) Indirect light

 In winter, keep compost barely moist; in summer, water freely and feed every 2–3 weeks. Repot established plants in spring when roots fill the pot, usually every 2–3 years.

 Take 5–7.5cm (2–3in) stem-tip cuttings in late spring and insert in equal parts moist peat and sharp sand. Place in 16–18°C (61–64°F). Alternatively, sow seeds in late winter or spring, in 16°C (61°F).

Euphorbia millii
Christ Plant, Christ Thorn, Crown of Thorns

Earlier known as *Euphorbia splendens*, this tender, semi-succulent, semi-prostrate shrub has a woody nature and spiny stems. They are sparsely clad in pear-shaped, mid-green leaves, with flowers formed of two kidney-shaped, crimson bracts (modified leaves) throughout the year, but mostly in winter.

 30–60cm (1–2ft)

 13°C (55°F) Full sun

 30–60cm (1–2ft)

 13–16°C (55–61°F) Full sun, or direct light without full sun

 In winter, keep compost barely moist; in summer, water freely and feed every 2 weeks. Repot in spring when roots fill the pot, usually every 2 years.

 Take 7.5cm (3in) tip-cuttings in midsummer. Allow cut ends to dry before inserting them in equal parts moist peat and sharp sand. Place in 16–18°C (61–64°F).

Hibiscus rosa-sinensis
Blacking Plant, China Rose, Chinese Hibiscus, Chinese Rose, Hawaiian Hibiscus, Rose of China, Shoe Black Plant

Tender shrub with short-lived flowers, 13cm (5in) wide, from upper leaf joints throughout summer. Normally, flowers are single and crimson, but semi-double and double forms are available in colours from creamy-white to pale yellow. The dwarf form, 'Cooperi', with crimson flowers and variegated leaves, is ideal for growing indoors.

 45–60cm (1½–2ft) in a pot

 7–10°C (45–50°F)
Full sun

 38–45cm (15–18in) in a pot

 13–21°C (55–70°F)
Direct light without full sun, or indirect light

 In winter, keep compost barely moist; in summer, water freely but ensure good drainage, and feed every 2 weeks. Repot in spring when roots fill the pot, usually every year when young.

 Take 7.5–10cm (3–4in) cuttings from non-flowering shoots in midsummer and insert in equal parts moist peat and sharp sand. Place in 18°C (64°F).

Hoya carnosa
Honey Plant, Porcelain Flower, Wax Plant

Vigorous evergreen climber with oval, fleshy, mid-green leaves. From early summer to early autumn it produces umbrella-like heads, 7.5cm (3in) wide, of fragrant, white to flesh-pink star-like flowers. When young, plants can be trained around a hoop 25–30cm (10–12in) wide, but later need more substantial supports. There are several forms, including some with variegated leaves.

 2.4–4.5m (8–15ft) after several years

 7–10°C (45–50°F)
Direct light without full sun

 Climber

 16–21°C (61–70°F)
Direct light without full sun, or indirect light

 In winter, keep compost slightly moist; in summer, water freely if compost is well drained. Feed every 3 weeks from late spring to late summer. In late spring, repot plants with congested roots, usually every 2–3 years.

 Take 7.5–10cm (3–4in) stem-cuttings during early and midsummer and insert in equal parts moist peat and sharp sand. Place in 16–18°C (61–64°F).

Jasminum polyanthum
Jasmine, Pink Jasmine, Poet's Jassamine
Slightly tender climber, with a twining nature and dark-green leaves formed of 5 or 7 leaflets. From early winter to late spring, it produces a wealth of strongly scented white, tubular flowers (pink when in bud) in lax clusters. When grown as a houseplant, it is usually bought twining around a circular, hooped framework, 25–30cm (10–12in) across. Later, and if transferred to a conservatory, it needs a large supporting framework.

 90cm–3m (3–10ft)

 10–13°C (50–55°F); survives temperatures down to 7°C (45°F), but is then reluctant to flower so early in the year Full sun

 Climber

 13–18°C (55–64°F) Direct light without full sun, or indirect light

 In early winter, keep compost moist and increase watering frequency as buds start to form; in summer, water freely. Feed every 2 weeks from when buds start to appear. Repot pot-bound plants after the flowers fade. Alternatively, plants in large pots can be top-dressed with fresh compost.

 Take 7.5–10cm (3–4in) stem-tip cuttings in late spring and insert in equal parts moist peat and sharp sand. Place in 16–18°C (61–64°F).

Justicia brandegeeana
False Hop Plant, Junta-de-cobra-pintada, Mexican Shrimp Plant, Shrimp Bush, Shrimp Plant
Earlier known as *Beloperone guttata*, this distinctive shrub-like, evergreen perennial has soft green leaves and shrimp-like flowers formed of colourful bracts and inconspicuous white flowers from spring to midwinter.

 45–60cm (1½–2ft), sometimes more

 7–13°C (45–55°F) Direct light without full sun

 30–45cm (1–1½ft), sometimes more

 13–24°C (55–75°F) Indirect light

 In winter, keep compost barely moist, especially if the temperature falls; in summer, water compost freely. From late spring to late summer, feed every 2–3 weeks. Repot in early spring when roots fill the pot, usually every 2–3 years. Alternatively, top-dress plants in large pots with fresh compost.

 Take 5–7.5cm (2–3in) cuttings in early spring and insert in equal parts moist peat and sharp sand. Place in 18–21°C (64–70°F).

INSECTIVOROUS HOUSEPLANTS

Insectivorous plants (insectivores) reveal how nature has adapted some plants to live in places where their roots cannot gain sufficient nutrients from the soil. Instead, adaptations allow them to trap and digest insects. Some, such as the Venus Fly Trap, use hinged jaws that snap shut when triggered by an insect, a few use sticky surfaces, and others have pitcher-like heads into which insects fall.

Insectivorous plants are not easy to grow indoors; they need to be watered with rainwater and kept in a humid atmosphere. They usually grow in marshy ground and need high humidity and indirect light. In winter, 10–13°C (50–55°F) suits them, with a few degrees higher in summer. They need light shade, especially in summer. Use clean rainwater to keep the compost slightly moist. If your home has a dry atmosphere, domed plastic covers create a humid environment for them.

FLY TRAPS

1 **Dionaea muscipula** Venus Fly Trap
Forms a rosette of light-green leaves with hinged jaws. When a fly wanders into the open jaws it touches trigger hairs that instantly close them. Digestive juices break down the insect's body and the plant absorbs the nutrients. Later, the hinged jaws open, ready to trap another fly.

STICKY-LEAVED PLANTS

Instead of jaws, these have sticky hairs and are known as sundews. These are a few of many different species.

2 **Drosera binata** Giant Fork-leaved Sundew
Leaves divide at their tops into 2 or 4 segments; sticky hairs trap and digest insects.

3 **Drosera capensis** Sundew
Leaf rosettes covered with red hairs trap and digest insects; purple flowers on stems up to 38cm (15in) high.

4 **Drosera rotundifolia** Round-leaved Sundew
Small plant, with long-stemmed round leaves covered with fine, red hairs; glands on the leaves exude clear drops of fluid resembling small dew drops.

PITCHER PLANTS (Hooded and Lidded)

5 **Darlingtonia californica** Californian Pitcher Plant, Cobra Lily, Cobra Orchid, Hooded Pitcher Plant
Hooded pitcher plant resembling a cobra's head; heavily veined, yellowish or pale green, up to 60cm (2ft) high.

6 **Nepenthes x coccinea** Pitcher Plant
Lidded type, with brightly coloured pitchers. Best positioned in indoor hanging-basket, or a pot on a shelf, so the pitchers hang freely. Insects fall in and are digested.

7 **Sarracenia flava** Huntsman's Horn, Trumpet Leaf, Umbrella Trumpets, Watches, Yellow Pitcher Plant
Long, yellow-green pitchers with purple or crimson veining in their throats. Each has an erect lid. Insects fall into the pitcher and are digested.

8 **Sarracenia purpurea** Huntsman's Cup, Indian Cup, Pitcher Plant, Side-saddle Flower
Purple and green pitchers (resembling raw meat) attract flies, which fall inside and are digested.

Pachystachys lutea
Lollipop Plant

This tender, shrub-like plant has golden-yellow, poker-like heads throughout summer and into autumn. Flowers appear above the dark-green, narrowly oval to lance-shaped leaves.

 38–45cm (15–18in)

 13°C (55°F); can survive temperatures down to 10°C (50°F) if compost is kept slightly dry. Direct light without full sun

 30–38cm (12–15in)

 13–21°C (55–70°F) Indirect light

 In winter, keep compost barely moist; in summer, water freely. Feed every 2 weeks from late spring to late summer. Repot when roots fill the pot, usually every year when young. Older plants can be top-dressed with fresh compost.

 Take 10–13cm (4–5in) stem-tip cuttings in spring or early summer and insert in equal parts moist peat and sharp sand. Place in 21°C (70°F).

Spathiphyllum wallisii
Peace Lily, Sail Plant, Spathe Flower

This evergreen perennial has bright-green, lance-shaped leaves borne on long, stiff, upright stems. White, arum-like flowers appear from mid-spring to late summer. The hybrid *Spathiphyllum* 'Mauna Loa' produces larger, more brightly coloured flowers.

 23–30cm (9–12in)

 10–13°C (50–55°F) Full sun

 30–38cm (12–15in)

 18–21°C (64–70°F) Direct light without full sun, or indirect light

 In winter, keep compost evenly moist; in summer, water freely. Feed with weak fertilizer every 10–14 days from mid-spring to late summer. Feed every 4–5 weeks during the rest of the year. Repot when roots fill the pot, usually every year.

 Divide congested plants in spring. Until established, place in 10–13°C (50–55°F).

Stephanotis floribunda
Floradora, Madagascar Jasmine, Wax Flower

This tender, evergreen twining, climbing shrub has dark-green, leathery, oval leaves about 7.5cm (3in) long. In summer and into autumn, it produces heads of up to 8 exquisitely scented, waxy-white flowers, 36mm (1½in) long. When young, it can be grown over a 25–30cm (10–12in) hoop-like frame; later more substantial support is needed.

 3m (10ft) when in a conservatory; initially, and when in a pot 15–20cm (6–8in) wide, it is much smaller — often no more than 45cm (18in) high

 10–13°C (50–55°F) Direct light without full sun

 18–21°C (64–70°F) Direct light without full sun, or indirect light

 Climber

 In winter, keep compost slightly moist; in summer, water freely but ensure it is well drained. Feed every 2–3 weeks from late spring to late summer. Repot in spring when roots fill the pot, initially every year, but later every 2–3 years.

 Take 10cm (4in) cuttings from side-shoots in late spring or early summer and insert in equal parts moist peat and sharp sand. Place in 21°C (70°F).

Streptocarpus x hybridus
Cape Primrose

These evergreen, tufted hybrids are derived from a wide range of streptocarpus species and well known for their long, spoon-shaped, mid-green and corrugated leaves. They bear foxglove-like flowers, 36–60mm (1½–2½in) long, in small clusters from early summer to autumn. The wide colour range includes white, red and purple. 'Constant Nymph' has satiny, bluish-purple flowers.

 20–30cm (8–12in)

 10–13°C (50–55°F) Direct light without full sun

 23–38cm (9–15in)

 13–15°C (55–59°F) Direct light without full sun

 In winter, keep compost just moist; in summer, water freely but ensure good drainage. Feed every 2–3 weeks from late spring to late summer. Repot in spring when roots fill the pot, usually every 2–3 years.

 Divide congested plants in spring, initially placing them in 10–13°C (50–55°F). Alternatively, take leaf-cuttings in midsummer and place in 13–16°C (55–61°F). Avoid high temperatures.

OTHER FLOWERING HOUSEPLANTS

Allamanda cathartica (Golden Trumpet): climber with golden-yellow flowers during summer amid long, leathery, glossy green leaves. Several superb cultivars, including 'Hendersonii' (large, orange-yellow flowers) and 'Grandiflora' (pale-yellow flowers).

Brunfelsia pauciflora (Yesterday, Today and Tomorrow): earlier known as *Brunfelsia calycina*, this evergreen shrub has mid-green, shiny leaves and fragrant, violet-purple flowers with white throats from spring to autumn.

Crossandra infundibuliformis (Firecracker Flower): earlier known as *Crossandra undulifolia*, this evergreen shrub has wavy-edged, dark-green leaves and clusters of orange-red flowers from spring to autumn.

Gardenia jasminoides (Cape Jasmine): earlier known as *Gardenia augusta*, this tender evergreen shrub has highly fragrant, waxy white flowers, 7.5cm (3in) wide, from early to late summer.

Ixora coccinea (Flame of the Woods, Burning Love, Jungle Geranium): evergreen shrub with large heads, up to 10cm (4in) across, packed with tubular flowers in red, pink, salmon, yellow or white throughout summer.

Justicia carnea (King's Crown, Brazilian Plume, Paradise Plant): earlier known as *Jacobinia carnea*, this evergreen shrub has plume-like heads of pink, tubular flowers in late summer and early autumn.

Mandevilla splendens: earlier known as *Diplandenia splendens*, this twining, evergreen shrub bears 15–20cm (6–8in) clusters of rose-pink, trumpet-shaped flowers from early to late summer, sometimes into early autumn.

Plumbago auriculata (Cape Leadwort): earlier known as *Plumbago capensis*, this evergreen climber has star-shaped, tubular, sky-blue flowers during summer and into autumn.

Below left: Plumbago auriculata (Cape Leadwort)

Below: Brunfelsia pauciflora (Yesterday, Today and Tomorrow)

FLOWERING POTPLANTS

Flowering potplants are the most widely grown of all indoor plants. Each year vast numbers are bought when their colourful display begins, then discarded when it is over. They make superb presents and many enthusiasts try to grow them for a second year, but the display is often disappointing.

 HEIGHT   **SPREAD**   **WINTER**   **SUMMER**   **CARE**   **PROPAGATION**

Achimenes hybrids
Cupid's Bower, Hot Water Plant, Monkey-faced Pansy, Mother's Tears, Widow's Tears

From early to late summer, these hybrids bear masses of trumpet-like flowers. Colours include white, pink, red, purple and blue. Each flower is short-lived, but soon replaced by others.

	30–38cm (12–15in)		Not applicable
	25–30cm (10–12in)		13–15°C (55–59°F) Direct light without full sun, or indirect light
	In summer, water freely but ensure compost is well drained, and feed every 2–3 weeks.		
	Plants can be raised from tuber-like rhizomes, but fresh plants are usually bought each year.		

Astilbe x *arendsii*
Perennial Spiraea

Astilbes are hardy herbaceous perennials, sometimes encouraged by nurserymen to flower indoors for about a month during late winter and early spring, which is earlier than their normal summer-flowering period outdoors. They have deep-green, fern-like leaves and flowers borne in plume-like heads in colours such as clear pink, dark red, salmon-red and white.

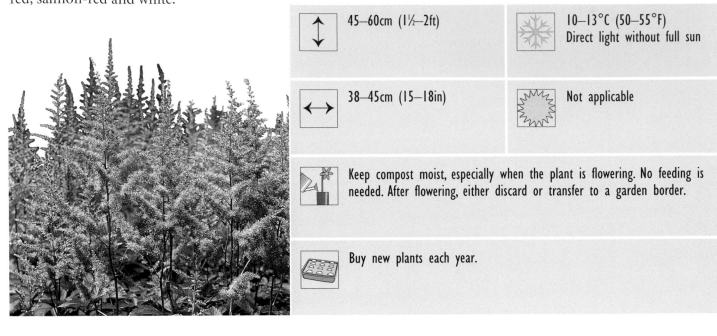

	45–60cm (1½–2ft)		10–13°C (50–55°F) Direct light without full sun
	38–45cm (15–18in)		Not applicable

Keep compost moist, especially when the plant is flowering. No feeding is needed. After flowering, either discard or transfer to a garden border.

Buy new plants each year.

Azalea indica
Azalea, Indian Azalea

Properly known as *Rhododendron simsii*, this small, bushy, evergreen shrub is encouraged by nurserymen to flower from mid- to late winter. The small, narrowly oval to pear-shaped, dark-green leaves create an attractive background for the funnel-shaped flowers. Colours include crimson, salmon, pink and white, in single- and double-flowered forms. There are also bicoloured forms.

	30–45cm (1–1½ft) when in a pot		10–15°C (50–59°F); avoid high temperatures. Direct light without full sun, or indirect light
	38–45cm (15–18in) when in a pot		Not applicable

Keep compost moist when the plant is flowering. No feeding is needed. After flowering, it can be planted in a garden.

Buy fresh plants each year.

Begonia x tuberhybrida
Hybrid Tuberous Begonia, Tuberous Begonia, Tuberous-rooted Begonia

Also known as *Begonia* Tuberhybrida Hybrids, these floriferous, tuberous-rooted plants have mid-green leaves and large, rose-like flowers from early summer to early autumn. Apart from being grown as houseplants, they can be planted in gardens for summer flowering. Individual flowers are 7.5–15cm (3–6in) across, in colours including scarlet, rose-pink, golden-yellow, crimson and orange.

 30–50cm (12–20in)

 Not applicable, unless increasing your own plants (*see* below)

 30–38cm (12–15in)

 13–18°C (55–64°F); avoid high temperatures Direct light without full sun, or indirect light

 When in flower, keep compost moist, but not waterlogged, and feed every 2–3 weeks.

 Buy fresh plants each year, or put tubers in boxes of moist peat in 18°C (64°F) in early or mid-spring. When shoots develop, transfer the tubers to individual pots and lower the temperature slightly to 13°C (55°F). Later, place in 13–18°C (55–64°F).

Calceolaria x herbeohybrida
Pocketbook Flower, Pouch Flower, Slipper Flower, Slipper Plant

These tender hybrids exhibit bushy growth and masses of pouch-like flowers from late spring to midsummer when indoors. Colours include shades of yellow, orange and red, either spotted or blotched in crimson.

 20–45cm (8–18in)

 Not applicable

 20–38cm (8–15in)

 10–15°C (50–59°F); avoid high temperatures Direct light without full sun

 When flowering, keep compost moist and feed every 2 weeks. Discard plants after flowering and replace the following year.

 Plants are biennial, raised from seed sown in midsummer and overwintered as young plants.

Celosia argentea 'Plumosa'

Feathered Amaranth, Plume Flower, Plumed Cock's Flower, Prince of Wales' Feather

Brightly coloured, pyramidal and feathery spires of flowers, 7.5–15cm (3–6in) high, appear from mid- to late summer. Colours include pink, yellow, crimson and amber. *Celosia argentea* 'Venezuela' is another attractive form (pictured below).

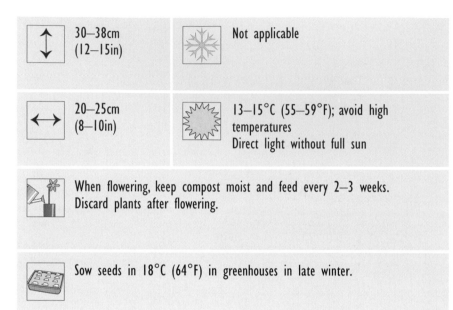

↕	30–38cm (12–15in)	❄	Not applicable
↔	20–25cm (8–10in)	☀	13–15°C (55–59°F); avoid high temperatures Direct light without full sun

When flowering, keep compost moist and feed every 2–3 weeks. Discard plants after flowering.

Sow seeds in 18°C (64°F) in greenhouses in late winter.

Chrysanthemum: all-year-round types

Popular flowering plants, available throughout the year either in pots or as cut flowers. Traditionally, they flower in late summer and through to midwinter, but young plants can be encouraged to flower at any time of the year by providing them with strict regimes of dark and light, and suitable temperatures. Nurseries also use chemicals to produce smaller plants. There are single- and double-flowered types in colours such as yellow, orange, red, pink and white.

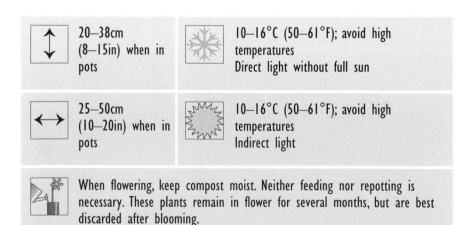

↕	20–38cm (8–15in) when in pots	❄	10–16°C (50–61°F); avoid high temperatures Direct light without full sun
↔	25–50cm (10–20in) when in pots	☀	10–16°C (50–61°F); avoid high temperatures Indirect light

When flowering, keep compost moist. Neither feeding nor repotting is necessary. These plants remain in flower for several months, but are best discarded after blooming.

Buy fresh plants throughout the year.

Cyclamen persicum
Alpine Violet, Cyclamen, Florist's Cyclamen, Persian Violet, Sow Bread

Popular houseplant sold from early autumn to spring. Shuttlecock-like flowers, some fragrant, appear above round, marble-coloured leaves. Colours include pink, white or red, and pastel shades.

 There are several strains, including standard (about 30cm (12in) high), intermediate (about 23cm (9in) high) and miniature (about 15cm (6in) high)

 13–15°C (55–59°F) from when buds show colour Direct light without full sun, or indirect light

 See above; most plants are about the same width as they are high

 AUTUMN SPRING 13–15°C (55–59°F) Indirect light

 When flowering or buds are showing colour, keep compost moist and feed every 2–3 weeks. Most plants are discarded after the flowers fade, but if you decide to keep the plant, reduce the amount of water, gradually drying off the corm (still in the compost and pot), and place in a cool, airy place. In late summer, repot into a clean pot and fresh compost. Water the compost and place in a cool, bright greenhouse. When shoots and leaves start to develop, slowly increase the temperature and amount of water.

 Plants can be raised from seeds, but this is best left to nurserymen as it takes 12–15 months to produce large plants.

Erica gracilis
Cape Heath, Winter-flowering Erica

Evergreen, ericaceous plant with spires of pale-green leaves and tubular to globe-shaped, rosy-purple flowers in autumn and winter. There is also a white-flowered form.

 30–45cm (1–1½ft), sometimes smaller

 5–7°C (41–45°F); avoid high temperatures Full sun, or direct light without full sun

 25–30cm (10–12in), sometimes smaller

 Not applicable

 Use lime-free water and keep compost moist but not waterlogged. No feeding is needed.

 Discard plants after flowering (though they can be planted outdoors in warm, temperate climates).

Erica x hiemalis
French Heather, White Winter Heather, Winter-flowering Erica
Sometimes listed as *Erica hyemalis*, this ericaceous shrub has mid-green, thread-like leaves. Tubular flowers, white with a pink flush, are borne in terminal clusters from late autumn to late winter.

 38–45cm (15–18in), some-times slightly more

 5–7°C (41–45°F); avoid high temperatures
Full sun, or direct light without full sun

 25–30cm (10–12in), some-times slightly more

 Not applicable

 Use lime-free water and keep compost moist but not waterlogged. No feeding is needed.

 Discard plants after flowering (though they can be planted outdoors in warm, temperate climates).

Euphorbia pulcherrima
Christmas Star, Lobster Plant, Mexican Flameleaf, Painted Leaf, Poinsettia
This well-known late autumn to late winter flowering houseplant has colourful, leaf-like bracts up to 15cm (6in) long, usually bright crimson, though scarlet, white, pink and cream forms are also available.

 30–45cm (12–18in)

 15–16°C (55–61°F); avoid high temperatures
Indirect light

 30–45cm (12–18in)

 Not applicable

 Keep compost evenly moist, but not waterlogged. No feeding is needed. Poinsettias can be kept from one year to another, but because nurserymen use chemicals to produce compact and dwarf plants, they may be larger the following year. In practical terms, plants are best discarded.

 Buy a new plant the following year.

Exacum affine
Arabian Violet, German Violet, Mexican Violet, Persian Violet

Bushy plant with small, glossy, oval leaves and fragrant, violet flowers with yellow stamens from mid- to late summer.

| ↕ | 15–25cm (6–10in) | ❄ | Not applicable |
| ↔ | 15–25cm (6–10in) | ☀ | 13–16°C (55–61°F); avoid high temperatures Direct light without full sun |

Keep compost moist, but not continually saturated. Feed every 10 days with weak liquid fertilizer from when buds show colour to when the flowers fade.

Discard plants after their flowers fade.

Hydrangea macrophylla
Common Hydrangea, French Hydrangea, Hortensia, House Hydrangea

There are two types of *Hydrangea macrophylla*: the Mop-head type (sometimes known as Hortensia, with large, round flower heads 15–20cm (6–8in) wide) and the Lacecaps (flat, more open heads, 10–15cm (4–6in) wide). The Mop-head type is grown as a houseplant, in colours including white, blue, pink and red. They are ideal for introducing colour to cool rooms during late spring and early summer. Most are bought when just beginning to show colour. Outdoors, they flower from midsummer to autumn.

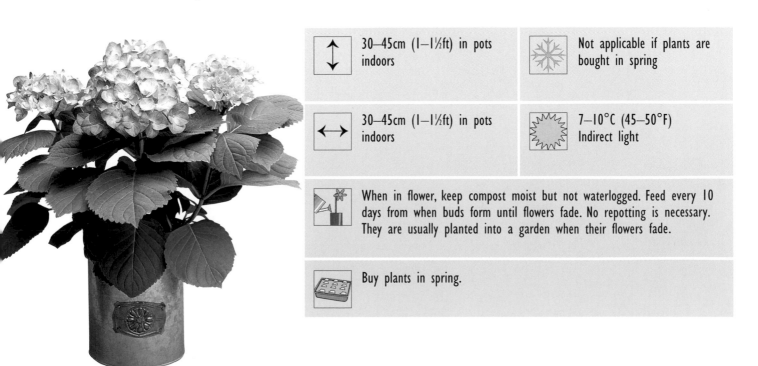

| ↕ | 30–45cm (1–1½ft) in pots indoors | ❄ | Not applicable if plants are bought in spring |
| ↔ | 30–45cm (1–1½ft) in pots indoors | ☀ | 7–10°C (45–50°F) Indirect light |

When in flower, keep compost moist but not waterlogged. Feed every 10 days from when buds form until flowers fade. No repotting is necessary. They are usually planted into a garden when their flowers fade.

Buy plants in spring.

Impatiens walleriana

Busy Lizzie, Patience Plant, Patient Lucy, Sultana, Zanzibar Balsam

Earlier known as *Impatiens sultani*, this is one of the most popular houseplants. It is sometimes classified as a flowering houseplant because it lives from one year to another, but usually becomes leggy and is replaced every year. It has flat-faced, 5-petalled flowers in colours such as pink, red, purple, orange and white. There are many hybrids in mixed colours, some with variegated leaves.

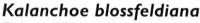

 30–60cm (1–2ft)

 13°C (55°F); it can withstand temperatures down to 7°C (45°F) if compost is kept slightly drier. Full sun, or direct light without full sun

 30–45cm (15–18in)

 16–18°C (61–64°F) Direct light without full sun

 Keep compost moist, but not waterlogged. From late spring to late summer, feed every week with weak liquid fertilizer. No repotting is needed if plants are discarded each year.

 Take 7.5–10cm (3–4in) stem-tip cuttings from late spring to late summer and insert in equal parts moist peat and sharp sand. Place in 16°C (61°F). Alternatively, buy fresh plants each year.

Kalanchoe blossfeldiana

Flaming Katy

Thick, succulent, dark-green leaves with scalloped edges. By manipulating periods of light and dark, combined with suitable temperatures, nurseries can produce flowering plants throughout the year. Each remains in flower for 6 weeks or more, then is discarded.
Colours include red, white, yellow, orange and lilac.

 20–25cm (8–10in)

 10–13°C (50–55°F) Full sun

 20–25cm (8–10in)

 13–18°C (55–64°F) Direct light without full sun, or indirect light

 Water compost thoroughly, but allow to dry out slightly between waterings. From when buds show colour, feed every 2–3 weeks.

 Buy plants throughout the year and discard after flowering.

Primula malacoides
Baby Primula, Fairy Primrose, Fairy Primula
Winter- and spring-flowering perennial, but usually grown as a greenhouse annual, it has pale-green, oval leaves. Whorls of star-like flowers appear in several colours – pink, carmine-red, white, lavender and white, with yellow eyes.

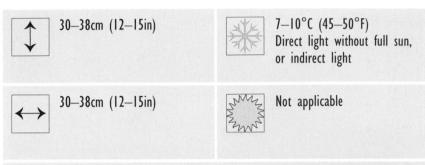

30–38cm (12–15in)	7–10°C (45–50°F) Direct light without full sun, or indirect light
30–38cm (12–15in)	Not applicable

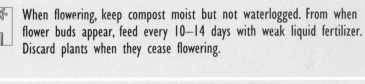

When flowering, keep compost moist but not waterlogged. From when flower buds appear, feed every 10–14 days with weak liquid fertilizer. Discard plants when they cease flowering.

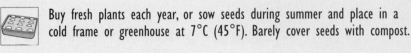

Buy fresh plants each year, or sow seeds during summer and place in a cold frame or greenhouse at 7°C (45°F). Barely cover seeds with compost.

Primula obconica
German Primrose, Poison Primrose
Although this is a greenhouse perennial, fresh plants are invariably raised as annuals, flowering from early winter to late spring. Clusters of flowers, 25mm (1in) wide, appear in pink, red, lilac or blue-purple. The light-green, oval to heart-shaped leaves form an attractive backdrop for the flowers, but can create painful rashes, especially on wrists and arms, especially when damp.

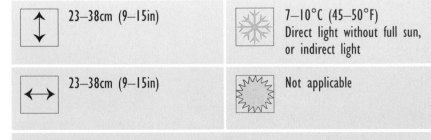

23–38cm (9–15in)	7–10°C (45–50°F) Direct light without full sun, or indirect light
23–38cm (9–15in)	Not applicable

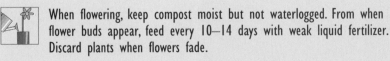

When flowering, keep compost moist but not waterlogged. From when flower buds appear, feed every 10–14 days with weak liquid fertilizer. Discard plants when flowers fade.

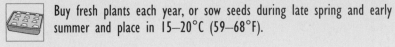

Buy fresh plants each year, or sow seeds during late spring and early summer and place in 15–20°C (59–68°F).

Primula sinensis
Chinese Primrose

Tender greenhouse perennial that is grown as a greenhouse annual in temperate areas. It has bright-green, lobed, tooth-edged hairy leaves. Flowers, 25–36mm (1–1½in) wide, are borne in clusters from midwinter to early spring. Some have frilly edges. Colours include white, pink, red, orange and purple. Like *Primula obconica*, the leaves can cause rashes on arms and wrists, especially when damp.

 25cm (10in)

 10°C (50°F); avoid high temperatures Direct light without full sun, or indirect light

 20–25cm (8–10in)

 Not applicable, unless raising your own plants from seeds (*see* below)

 When flowering, keep compost moist but not waterlogged. From when flower buds appear, feed every 10–14 days with weak liquid fertilizer. No repotting is necessary.

 Sow seeds in seed-trays from late spring to midsummer. Place in a cold frame at 7°C (45°F). Barely cover seeds with compost.

Saintpaulia ionantha
African Violet, Usambava Violet

Small, evergreen plant with velvet-textured, dark- to mid-green, heart-shaped leaves and small purple, violet-like flowers with bright golden-yellow eyes, mainly from early summer to early autumn. There are many strains and nowadays you can have African Violets in flower at any time of year. The range of flower types includes single, semi-double, double, frilled, star, bicolor and multicolour. Some have all-green leaves, others are variegated, spoon-edged or serrated. There are also trailing types.

 About ⅔ of the spread (*see* below)

 15–18°C (59–64°F) Full sun, or direct light without full sun

 Micro-miniatures: less than 7.5cm (3in); miniatures: 7.5–15cm (3–6in); semi-miniatures: 15–20cm (6–8in); standard varieties: 38cm (15in); large varieties: more than 38cm (15in)

 15–18°C (59–64°F) Direct light without full sun

 Keep compost moist in summer and winter, but not continually saturated. From late spring to late summer, feed every 2 weeks with weak liquid fertilizer. No repotting is necessary.

 Take leaf-stem cuttings during summer and insert leaf-stems in equal parts moist peat and sharp sand. Place in 18–24°C (64–70°F).

Schizanthus pinnatus
Butterfly Flower, Poor Man's Orchid

This bushy annual is grown as a half-hardy annual in temperate climates. During spring and early summer, plants produce masses of orchid-like flowers amid pale-green, almost fern-like leaves. Flower colours include yellow, purple and rose, with attractive markings and spots. These plants can also be grown outdoors in warm, temperate climates, when they flower from mid-summer to early autumn.

 30–75cm (1–2½ft) – range of cultivars

 7–10°C (45–50°F)
Full sun

 25–38cm (10–15in) – range of cultivars

 7–13°C (45–55°F)
Direct light without full sun

 Keep compost moist, especially when the plant is flowering. From when flower buds show colour to when they fade, feed every 10 days with weak liquid fertilizer. Discard after flowering.

 Sow seeds in late summer in seed-trays. Place in 15–20°C (59–68°F).

Senecio cruentus
Cineraria, Florist's Cineraria

Botanically known as *Pericallis* x *hybrida*, and earlier as *Cineraria cruenta* and *Cineraria* x *hybrida*, it produces masses of large, daisy-like flowers in flat or domed heads from late winter to midsummer. White, blue, purple, pink and red flowers appear above mid-green, somewhat heart-shaped leaves up to 20cm (8in) across. Flower shapes vary. Grandiflora types have individual flowers 5–7.5cm (2–3in) wide on plants 45–60cm (1½–2ft) high; Multiflora Nana types have flowers 25–50mm (1–2in) wide on plants 23–38cm (9–15in) high; double-flowered forms have flowers about 5cm (2in) wide on plants 30–60cm (1–2ft) high. Stellata types have star-like flowers 25–36mm (1–1½ in) wide on plants about 60cm (2ft) high.

 See above

 10–15°C (50–59°F); avoid high temperatures.
Direct light without full sun

 See above; most plants are about the same width as they are high

 10–15°C (50–59°F); avoid high temperatures.
Indirect light

 Keep compost moist, especially when the plant is flowering. Feeding is not usually necessary, but you can produce larger plants by giving weak liquid fertilizer every 2 weeks from when the flowers show colour. Discard plants when flowers fade.

 Buy fresh plants each year.

Sinningia cardinalis
Cardinal Flower

Earlier known as *Rechsteineria cardinalis* and *Gesneria cardinalis*, this tuberous-rooted plant has spectacular, hooded, bright scarlet flowers with paler throats. They are 5cm (2in) long, borne in terminal clusters from early to late summer. The velvet-surfaced leaves are broadly oval and 10cm (4in) long.

 23–45cm (9–18in)

 25–30cm (10–12in)

 Not applicable

 16–18°C (61–64°F) Direct light without full sun, or indirect light

 Keep compost moist but not waterlogged while the plant is flowering. If you decide not to discard the plant when flowers fade and leaves turn yellow, gradually cease watering, remove dead leaves and flowers and store tubers in 13°C (55°F) in a dry, airy place. Restart into growth in spring in 21°C (70°F), slowly increasing the amount of water. No feeding is necessary.

 Buy fresh plants each year.

Sinningia speciosa
Brazilian Gloxinia, Florist's Gloxinia, Gloxinia, Violet Slipper Gloxinia

Earlier known as *Gloxinia speciosa*, this tuberous-rooted plant has fleshy, velvety, almost stemless, large, oblong, dark-green leaves up to 20cm (8in) long. Bell-shaped flowers, 5–10cm (2–4in) long and 7.5cm (3in) across, appear from late spring to late summer. Colours include violet and purple. There are several named cultivars in white, red, pink and purple, some with coloured or crimped edges. Most Gloxinias are bought when buds are just showing colour, and flowers continue for 8 or more weeks.

 23–35cm (9–14in)

 25–30cm (10–12in)

 Not applicable if plants are bought when in flower

 18°C (64°F) Indirect light

 From late spring to late summer, keep compost moist, but not waterlogged. Feed every 2 weeks with weak liquid fertilizer from when the buds show colour.

 In late winter, place dormant tubers in boxes of moist peat in 21°C (70°F). When shoots are about 36mm (1½in) high, pot up each tuber into an individual pot. However, it is simpler to buy fresh plants each year.

Smithiantha hybrids
Temple Bells

Tender, rhizomatous hybrids mainly derived from *Smithiantha cinnabarina* and *Smithiantha zebrina*. They have dark-green, heart-shaped leaves and many pendulous, long and bell-shaped, foxglove-like flowers in shades of white, yellow-red, orange and pink (many with purple markings). They are borne on large, pyramidal heads from early to late summer.

 45–60cm (1½–2ft)

 18–21°C (64–70°F)
Full sun

 30–45cm (1–1½ft)

 18–21°C (64–70°F)
Direct light without full sun, or indirect light

 From early to late summer, keep compost moist, but not waterlogged. No feeding is necessary.

 Divide congested rhizomes at potting time, from late winter to late spring and place in 18–21°C (64–70°F). Alternatively, take leaf cuttings in late spring or early summer and place in 21°C (70°F).

Thunbergia alata
Black-eyed Susan

Well known climbing garden plant in temperate climates but also superb indoors for creating a colourful screen. During summer, it has white, yellow, or orange flowers, each with a black eye, amid oval, mid-green leaves.

 90cm–1.2m
(3–4ft)

 Not applicable

 45–60cm (1½–2ft),
sometimes more

 10–16°C (50–61°F); avoid high temperatures
Direct light without full sun

 In summer, keep compost moist but not waterlogged. From when the buds show colour, feed with weak liquid fertilizer every 10 days.

 Either buy plants in late spring or early summer, or sow seeds in seed-trays in early spring. Place in 16–18°C (61–64°F).

OTHER FLOWERING POTPLANTS

Begonia – Elatior types (Elatior Begonias, Hiemalis Begonias, Large-flowered Winter Begonias): properly known as hybrids between *Begonia socotrana* and *Begonia* x *tuberhybrida*, these are similar to the Lorraine types, but with larger flowers, up to 5cm (2in) wide. Colours include yellow, white, pink and salmon-orange, in single- and double-flowered forms.

Begonia – Lorraine types (Lorraine Begonias): properly known as hybrids between *Begonia socotrana* (Grape-leaf Begonia) and *Begonia dregei* (Maple-leaf Begonia), these floriferous plants have round, mid-green leaves about 7.5cm (3in) across and masses of deep-pink flowers, 25mm (1in) wide, during mid- and late winter. Several cultivars. Colours include salmon-orange, white, deep orange and yellow.

Begonia semperflorens (Wax Begonia): bushy and floriferous plant grown as a half-hardy annual in temperate climates and planted into flowerbeds. Colours from white, through pink and red to scarlet during summer.

Browallia speciosa (Bush Violet): small, bushy, tender plant, grown as a half-hardy annual, with tubular, violet-shaped flowers from early summer to early autumn.

Catharanthus roseus (Madagascar Periwinkle): earlier known as *Vinca rosea*, this evergreen sub-shrub bears white, lavender or rose flowers with darker-coloured throats throughout summer and into early autumn.

Chrysanthemum frutescens (Marguerite): now properly known as *Argyranthemum frutescens*, this perennial sub-shrubby plant has branching stems and grey-green, fern-like leaves. Single, white or pale-yellow flowers, about 5cm (2in) wide, appear throughout summer.

Chrysanthemum x ***morifolium*** (Pot Chrysanthemum): now often known as *Dendranthema* x *grandiflorum*, this is a popular houseplant with dark-green, lobed leaves up to 13cm (5in) long. Single or double flowers, 5–10cm (2–4in wide), on plants about 30cm (12in) high.

Gerbera jamesonii (Barberton Daisy, Transvaal Daisy): large, daisy-like flowers from early to late summer. Mid-green leaves, 15cm (6in) long, are deeply lobed and woolly beneath. Single- and double-flowered forms in many colours, including yellow, orange, pink, red and white. The centre of each flower forms a large yellow disc.

Below left: Begonia – Elatior type
Below: Chrysanthemum

CACTI AND OTHER SUCCULENTS

Cacti and succulents are usually grouped together, but they are botanically different. All cacti, with the exception of pereskias, are succulents, but not all succulents are cacti. Cacti belong exclusively to the Cactaceae family and are characterized by having areoles (like small pincushions) from which spines, short hooks or woolly hairs grow. Most cacti are native to dry regions, but a few live in the branches of trees in forests. Both cacti and other succulents are popular indoors and many bear flowers.

When should you repot cacti and other succulents? This is usually done in late spring or early summer but the frequency depends on the stage and speed of growth of the plant. Although repotting is required annually when young, later it is only necessary when roots fill the pot, which can be every 2–3 years. Even then, repot only if essential and into an only slightly larger pot. Indeed, most cacti grow quite well in small pots. With succulents, use a shallow pot rather than a deep one.

Agave filifera
Thread Agave

This succulent has white threads along the edges of its tapering dark-green, leathery leaves, which are 25mm (1in) wide. Eventually (though seldom seen on houseplants), it develops a long flower spike of purple and green bell-like flowers.

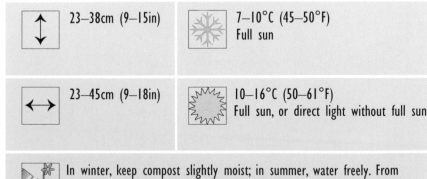

↕	23–38cm (9–15in)	❄	7–10°C (45–50°F) Full sun
↔	23–45cm (9–18in)	☀	10–16°C (50–61°F) Full sun, or direct light without full sun

 In winter, keep compost slightly moist; in summer, water freely. From spring to late summer, feed every 2 weeks with weak liquid fertilizer.

 Remove offsets in spring, allow to dry for a few days, then transfer to small pots. Place in 15°C (59°F), lightly shading until established.

Agave victoriae-reginae

This succulent plant has a rosette of dark-green leaves, 15cm (6in) long, with irregular white markings. Each leaf is keeled and tipped with a spine. Plants do not bloom until at least 10 years old, with cream flowers on tall stems.

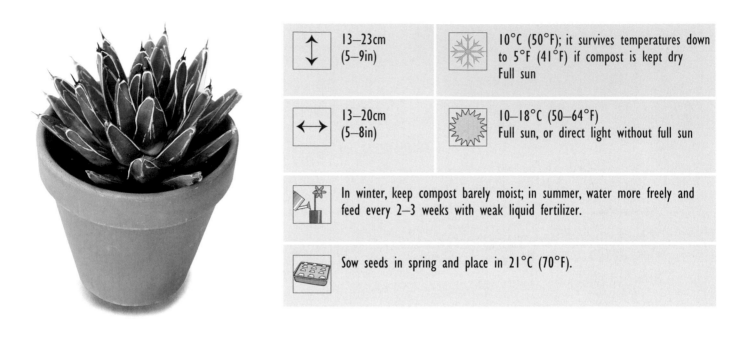

↕	13–23cm (5–9in)	❄	10°C (50°F); it survives temperatures down to 5°F (41°F) if compost is kept dry Full sun
↔	13–20cm (5–8in)	☀	10–18°C (50–64°F) Full sun, or direct light without full sun

In winter, keep compost barely moist; in summer, water more freely and feed every 2–3 weeks with weak liquid fertilizer.

Sow seeds in spring and place in 21°C (70°F).

Aloe variegata

Kanniedood Aloe, Partridge-breasted Aloe, Partridge-breasted Pheasant's Wings, Pheasant's Wings, Tiger Aloe

Succulent plant with dark-green leaves, irregularly cross-banded and blotched white. The stiff, keeled, somewhat triangular leaves arise in overlapping ranks. During summer, the plant develops orange flowers on stems about 25cm (10in) long.

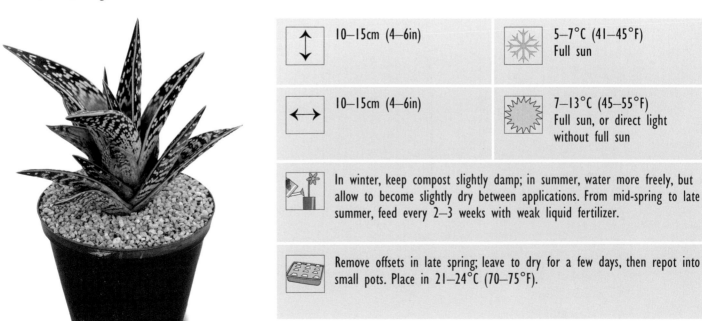

↕	10–15cm (4–6in)	❄	5–7°C (41–45°F) Full sun
↔	10–15cm (4–6in)	☀	7–13°C (45–55°F) Full sun, or direct light without full sun

In winter, keep compost slightly damp; in summer, water more freely, but allow to become slightly dry between applications. From mid-spring to late summer, feed every 2–3 weeks with weak liquid fertilizer.

Remove offsets in late spring; leave to dry for a few days, then repot into small pots. Place in 21–24°C (70–75°F).

Aporocactus flagelliformis
Rat's Tail Cactus, Rattail Cactus

Forest cactus with long, spine-clad, mid-green stems, 12mm (½ in) wide and up to 90cm (3ft) long. It bears funnel-shaped, magenta flowers during mid- and late spring.

↕	5–7.5cm (2–3in)	❄	7°C (45°F) Full sun
↔	5–7.5cm (2–3in), then trailing 75cm (2½ft) or more	☀	10–18°C (50–64°F) Direct light without full sun

In winter, keep compost slightly moist; in early spring, increase the amount of water. Feed every 2 weeks from when buds reveal colour to the onset of late summer. Repot plants after their flowers fade — usually every year.

Take 7.5cm (3in) stem-cuttings in early and midsummer. Allow the stem ends to dry, insert in sandy compost and place in 21°C (70°F).

Astrophytum asterias
Sand Dollar, Sand Dollar Cactus, Sea Urchin Cactus, Silver Dollar

Cactus with a grey-green, flattened, hemisphere-like body covered with white spots and revealing 8 spineless ribs. During early and midsummer it produces pale, shiny yellow flowers.

↕	25–30mm (1–1¼in)	❄	5–10°C (41–50°F) Full sun
↔	5–7.5cm (2–3in)	☀	10–21°C (50–70°F) Full sun, or direct light without full sun

In winter, keep compost dry; in summer, water whenever it becomes dry. Feed every 2 weeks from when buds show colour to late summer.

Sow seeds in spring, in 24–27°C (75–80°F).

Astrophytum capricorne
Goat's Horn Cactus

Initially, this cactus has a globular body, later cylindrical. It is light green, with 7–8 prominent ribs from which brownish-black, curved spines develop. The body is dappled with white, flaky scales. From early to midsummer, it produces yellow flowers, 5cm (2in) wide, with reddish centres.

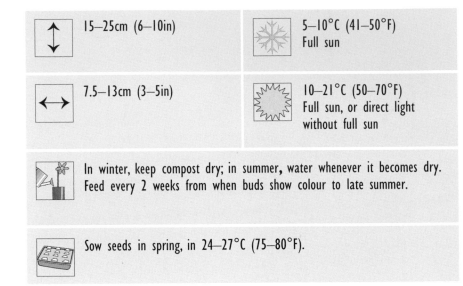

↕ 15–25cm (6–10in)	❄ 5–10°C (41–50°F) Full sun
↔ 7.5–13cm (3–5in)	☀ 10–21°C (50–70°F) Full sun, or direct light without full sun

In winter, keep compost dry; in summer, water whenever it becomes dry. Feed every 2 weeks from when buds show colour to late summer.

Sow seeds in spring, in 24–27°C (75–80°F).

Astrophytum myriostigma
Bishop's Cap Cactus, Bishop's Hood, Monk's-hood

When young, this cactus has a globular body, later cylindrical. It is dark green, almost grey, with silvery scales and 5–6 prominent ribs running up its body. During early and midsummer it bears sweet-scented yellow flowers up to 36mm (1½ in) wide.

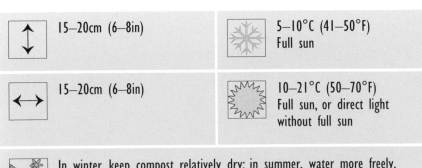

↕ 15–20cm (6–8in)	❄ 5–10°C (41–50°F) Full sun
↔ 15–20cm (6–8in)	☀ 10–21°C (50–70°F) Full sun, or direct light without full sun

In winter, keep compost relatively dry; in summer, water more freely. Feed every 2 weeks from when buds show colour to late summer.

Sow seeds in spring, in 24–27°C (75–80°F).

Cephalocereus senilis
Old Man Cactus

This desert cactus is tall in the wild but much smaller as a houseplant. It has a pale-green body and yellow spines, completely covered by long white hairs. White flowers do not usually appear when grown indoors.

 20–60cm (8–24in) when grown indoors

 7–10°C (45–50°F) Full sun

 7.5–15cm (3–6in) when grown indoors

 10–24°C (50–75°F) Full sun, or direct light without full sun

 In winter, keep compost barely moist; in summer, water freely and feed every 2 weeks.

 As it ages the lower part becomes unattractive; cut off the top, allow the cut to dry for a few days, then insert in sandy compost, preferably in spring or summer, and place in 15–18°C (59–64°F).

Cereus peruvianus (Cereus uruguayanus)
Apple Cactus, Column Cactus, Peruvian Apple, Peruvian Apple Cactus

This columnar cactus has a bluish-green, ribbed column and stout, brown spines. Eventually, it produces large, scented, white, funnel-shaped flowers, 5–7.5cm (2–3in) wide. *Cereus peruvianus monstrosus,* sometimes listed as *Cereus 'Monstrosus'* (pictured), is an unusual form that is much smaller than the species and has attractively distorted, branched stems with irregular ribs.

 60–90cm (2–3ft) when grown indoors

 5–7°C (41–45°F) Full sun

 7.5–15cm (3–6in) when grown indoors

 10–24°C (50–75°F) Full sun, or direct light without full sun

 In winter, keep compost barely moist; in summer, water freely. From late spring to late summer, feed every 2 weeks with weak liquid fertilizer.

 When plants become too large, cut off the top, allow the cut surface to dry slightly and insert in sandy compost, preferably in spring or summer, and place in 15–18°C (59–64°F). The lower part is usually discarded.

Chamaecereus silvestrii (Echinopsis chamaecereus)
Peanut Cactus
Desert cactus with finger-like green stems that create a sprawling plant with a profusion of brilliant scarlet flowers during spring and early summer.

 10–15cm (4–6in)

 2–7°C (35–45°F); it survives lower temperatures, but the compost must be kept dry. Avoid high winter temperatures, which discourage flower bud formation. Full sun

 13–15cm (5–6in), then spreading

 10–27°C (50–80°F) Full sun, or direct light without full sun

 In winter, keep compost barely moist; in summer, water freely. From late spring to late summer, feed every 2 weeks with weak liquid fertilizer.

 Short pieces of stem can be removed in spring, inserted in sandy compost and placed in 15–18°C (59–64°F).

Cleistocactus strausii
Silver Torch
Desert cactus with a columnar nature, densely covered in short, white spines that impart a silvery gleam. Mature specimens sometimes produce tubular, scarlet flowers, 7.5cm (3in) long, during mid- and late summer.

 90cm–1.8m (3–6ft)

 5–10°C (41–50°F) Full sun

 10–13cm (4–5in); sometimes forms a clump

 10–24°C (50–75°F) Full sun

 In winter, keep compost barely moist; in summer, water freely. Throughout summer, feed every 2 weeks with liquid fertilizer.

 Sow seeds in spring and place in 21°C (70°F).

Cotyledon orbiculata
Pig's Ears

Succulent, evergreen, shrubby plant with branching stems and large, grey-green leaves, 13cm (5in) long and 5–7.5cm (2–3in) wide, with red edges. It produces tubular, yellow and red flowers during midsummer.

 60–90cm (2–3ft)

 10–13°C (50–55°F); survives temperatures down to 5°C (41°F) if compost is kept dry. Full sun

 38–60cm (15–24in)

 13–21°C (55–70°F) Full sun, or direct light without full sun

 In winter, water sparingly, especially if temperature is low; in summer, water freely but ensure good drainage. From late spring to late summer, feed every 2 weeks with weak liquid fertilizer.

 Remove one or two leaves in early summer, allow the cut surface to dry and insert in sandy compost. Place in 16°C (61°F).

Crassula muscosa
Moss Cypress, Princess Pine, Rattail Cypress, Toy Cypress, Watch-chain Cypress

Also known as *Crassula lycopodioides*, this succulent resembles a miniature cypress. It has branching stems clothed in small, fleshy, overlapping, scale-like and triangular, mid- to dark-green leaves.

 15–25cm (6–10in)

 7–10°C (45–50°F) Direct light without full sun

 10–15cm (4–6in)

 10–15°C (50–59°F) Direct light without full sun

 In winter, keep compost slightly moist; in summer, water more freely and feed every 2–3 weeks with weak liquid fertilizer.

 Divide congested plants when being repotted and place in 10°C (50°F).

Crassula perfolata var. falcata (Crassula falcata)
Airplane Plant, Airplane Propeller Plant, Propeller Plant, Scarlet Paint Brush, Sickle Plant
Shrubby, succulent with thickened stems and blue-green, fleshy leaves. The clusters of orange-red flowers during summer give the plant its common name: 7.5cm (3in) wide, they look like airplane propellers from above.

 38–60cm (15–24in)

 7–13°C (45–55°F); it survives temperatures down to 5°C (41°F) if compost is kept relatively dry. Full sun

 25–30cm (10–12in)

 13–21°C (55–70°F) Full sun, or direct light without full sun

 In winter, keep compost barely moist but do not allow it to dry out; in summer, water more freely. Feed with weak liquid fertilizer every 2 weeks from late spring to late summer.

 Take leaf-cuttings in spring, insert in sandy compost and place in 24°C (70°F).

Echeveria derenbergii
Baby Echeveria, Painted Lady
Succulent with broad, spoon-shaped, pale-green leaves with red edges and covered with a white bloom. The leaves are tightly packed to form an attractive rosette. Later, it forms a cushion, with freely developing offsets. During midsummer, it bears orange-yellow, bell-shaped flowers on stems about 7.5cm (3in) high.

 5–7.5cm (2–3in)

 5–7°C (41–45°F); avoid high temperatures Full sun

 7.5–13cm (3–5in)

 10–21°C (50–70°F) Full sun, or direct light without full sun

 In winter, keep compost slightly moist; in summer, water freely. From late spring to late summer, feed every 2 weeks with weak liquid fertilizer.

 Take leaf-cuttings in late spring and insert in sandy compost. Place in 15–18°C (59–64°F).

Echeveria setosa
Firecracker Plant, Mexican Firecracker
Stemless succulent with a compact nature and dark-green leaves densely covered with white hairs. During spring, it develops orange-red flowers on stems up to 10cm (4in) high.

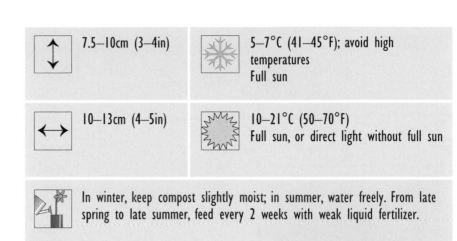

↕ 7.5–10cm (3–4in)	❄ 5–7°C (41–45°F); avoid high temperatures Full sun
↔ 10–13cm (4–5in)	☀ 10–21°C (50–70°F) Full sun, or direct light without full sun

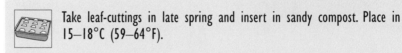

In winter, keep compost slightly moist; in summer, water freely. From late spring to late summer, feed every 2 weeks with weak liquid fertilizer.

Take leaf-cuttings in late spring and insert in sandy compost. Place in 15–18°C (59–64°F).

Echinocactus grusonii
Barrel Cactus, Golden Ball, Golden Ball Cactus, Golden Barrel Cactus
A slow-growing cactus, primarily grown for its barrel-like shape, it is covered with golden-yellow, awl-shaped spines. Small, yellow flowers appear on very large plants when positioned in full sun.

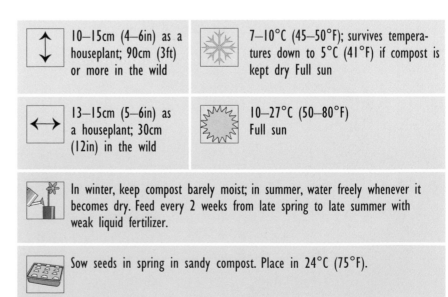

↕ 10–15cm (4–6in) as a houseplant; 90cm (3ft) or more in the wild	❄ 7–10°C (45–50°F); survives temperatures down to 5°C (41°F) if compost is kept dry Full sun
↔ 13–15cm (5–6in) as a houseplant; 30cm (12in) in the wild	☀ 10–27°C (50–80°F) Full sun

In winter, keep compost barely moist; in summer, water freely whenever it becomes dry. Feed every 2 weeks from late spring to late summer with weak liquid fertilizer.

Sow seeds in spring in sandy compost. Place in 24°C (75°F).

Echinocereus knippelianus

This desert cactus has deep-green branching stems formed of 5 ribs, with short, bristly spines along them. Pale-pink flowers, about 6cm (2½in) wide, appear in clusters during spring and summer.

↕ 7.5–10cm (3–4in)	❄ 5°C (41°F) Full sun
↔ 5cm (2in), but then forms a clump	☀ 10–18°C (50–64°F) Full sun
In winter, keep compost relatively dry; in summer, water freely and feed every 2 weeks with weak liquid fertilizer.	
Sow seeds in spring, placing them in 21°C (70°F).	

Echinocereus pectinatus

Cabeza del Viego, Old Man's Cap

Desert cactus with a cylindrical nature, formed of a green stem with 25 ribs covered with clusters of small, comb-like white spines. During early summer it bears cerise-pink flowers, 7.5cm (3in) long, that open to form wide bells.

↕ 15–20cm (6–8in)	❄ 5°C (41°F) Full sun
↔ 7.5cm (3in), branching and spreading	☀ 10–18°C (50–64°F) Full sun
In winter, keep compost relatively dry; in summer, water freely and feed every 2 weeks with weak liquid fertilizer.	
Sow seeds in spring, placing them in 21°C (70°F).	

Echinopsis eyriesii
Sea Urchin Cactus

This cactus is initially globular, but later elongated and branching. It has 15 prominent ribs clothed in short, dark-brown spines. It is mainly grown for its scented pure-white flowers, 15cm (6in) long, which open during summer evenings. Of many hybrids, perhaps the most popular is *Echinopsis* 'Green Gold', with golden-yellow flowers.

	15cm (6in) or more	2–5°C (35–41°F); avoid high temperature to ensure the plant flowers well the following summer. Full sun
	7.5–13cm (3–5in)	10–21°C (50–70°F) Full sun, or direct light without full sun

 In winter, keep compost relatively dry; in summer, water freely. From late spring to late summer, feed every 2 weeks with weak liquid fertilizer.

 Remove offsets in spring or early summer; allow cut surfaces to dry, insert in sandy compost and place in 15–18°C (59–64°F).

Epiphyllum ackermannii
Orchid Cactus, Pond Lily Cactus

Now known as *Nopalxochia ackermanii*, this forest cactus has leaning stems that need support when it is flowering – mainly in late spring and early summer, sometimes into midsummer. Many plants sold as *Epiphyllum ackermanii* are hybrids, which are easier to grow than the species. Hybrids are divided into two types: those with red or scarlet flowers, often 10–15cm (4–6in) wide; and those with yellow or white flowers, 10cm (4in) wide, which open during evenings (many reveal a sweet scent).

	60–90cm (2–3ft)	10°C (50°F) in early to late winter; from late winter to mid-spring, increase this to 13°C (55°F). Direct light without full sun
	25–30cm (10–12in)	13–21°C (55–70°F); from late summer to early winter, maintain 10–13°C (50–55°F). Direct light without full sun

From early to late winter, keep compost lightly moist, never letting it dry out. From late winter to early spring, slowly increase the amount of water. From mid-spring to late summer, keep compost moist but not waterlogged. From late summer to early winter, keep compost moist, watering when it shows signs of becoming dry. From when the flower buds start to form to when the last flower fades, feed every 2 weeks with weak, high-potash liquid fertilizer. Epiphyllums flower best when slightly pot-bound, but every 3 years repot them a short while after the last flower fades.

 During midsummer, take 13–15cm (5–6in) cuttings. Allow the cuts to dry for a few days, then insert in sandy compost and place in 21°C (70°F).

Euphorbia obesa
Gingham Golfball, Living Baseball, Turkish Temple

This spineless succulent has a greyish-green body and purple patterning. It is spherical at first, later cylindrical. It produces sweet-scented, bell-shaped green flowers during summer.

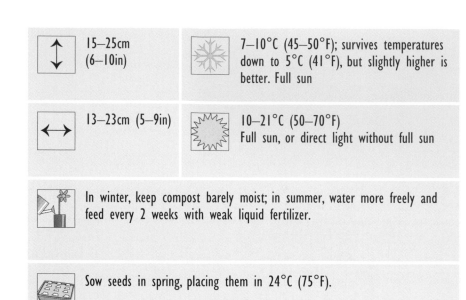

↕ 15–25cm (6–10in)	❄ 7–10°C (45–50°F); survives temperatures down to 5°C (41°F), but slightly higher is better. Full sun
↔ 13–23cm (5–9in)	☀ 10–21°C (50–70°F) Full sun, or direct light without full sun

In winter, keep compost barely moist; in summer, water more freely and feed every 2 weeks with weak liquid fertilizer.

Sow seeds in spring, placing them in 24°C (75°F).

Faucaria tigrina
Tiger Jaws

Stemless succulent with 4–5 pairs of grey-green, jaw-like leaves smothered in white dots. Each leaf has edges formed of 9–10 teeth. Golden-yellow flowers, about 5cm (2in) across, appear during summer and into early autumn.

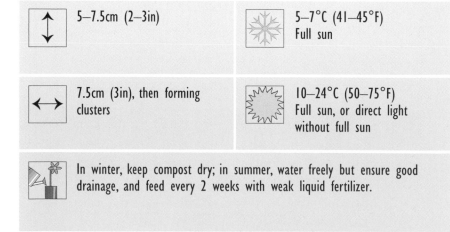

↕ 5–7.5cm (2–3in)	❄ 5–7°C (41–45°F) Full sun
↔ 7.5cm (3in), then forming clusters	☀ 10–24°C (50–75°F) Full sun, or direct light without full sun

In winter, keep compost dry; in summer, water freely but ensure good drainage, and feed every 2 weeks with weak liquid fertilizer.

 Sow seeds in spring and place in 21°C (70°F).

Ferocactus acanthodes

Sometimes known as *Ferocactus cylindraceus*, this well-armed desert cactus has a spherical body, becoming elongated with age, with up to 23 ribs on its glaucous green body. Spines grow from raised grey, woolly areoles. The centre spine of each group is long, red and hooked. Yellow flowers, about 5cm (2in) long, only appear on mature plants.

↕ 30–45cm (12–18in), sometimes 90cm (3ft) in a conservatory	❄ 5–7°C (41–45°F) Full sun
↔ 10–15cm (4–6in)	☀ 10–21°C (50–70°F) Full sun, or direct light without full sun
🌼 In winter, keep compost dry; in summer, water more frequently and feed every 2 weeks with weak liquid fertilizer.	
Sow seeds in spring and place in 24°C (75°F).	

Ferocactus horridus

Also known as *Ferocactus peninsulae*, this fearsome-looking, globular, glaucous green cactus has 12 ribs covered in groups of strong, reddish spines. The longest spine in each group is flattened and hooked at its tip. Yellow flowers sometimes appear during summer, but only on mature plants.

↕ 10–13cm (4–5in)	❄ 5°C (41°F) Full sun
↔ 10cm (4in)	☀ 5–24°C (41–75°F) Full sun
🌼 In winter, keep compost dry; in summer, water more frequently, allowing the compost to become dry between waterings, and feed every 2 weeks with weak liquid fertilizer.	
Sow seeds in spring and place in 24°C (75°F).	

Gasteria verrucosa (Gasteria carinata var. verrucosa)

Ox Tongue, Rice Gasteria, Wart Gasteria, Warty Aloe

This succulent has tapering, dark-green leaves 13–15cm (5–6in) long. They are borne in pairs, one above each other, and are smothered with white, wart-like blotches.

 13–15cm (5–6in)

 5–10°C (41–50°F)
Full sun

 13–23cm (5–9in)

 10–18°C (50–64°F)
Full sun

 In winter, keep compost barely moist, but give more water if temperature rises dramatically; in summer, water freely but ensure good drainage, and feed every 2 weeks with weak liquid fertilizer.

 Divide congested plants when repotting in spring and place in 10°C (50°F).

Glottiphyllum linguiforme

Succulent with thick, tongue-like, shiny green leaves about 5cm (2in) long. In autumn and early winter, it bears golden-yellow flowers that open on sunny days and close at night.

 5–7.5cm (2–3in)

 5°C (41°F)
Full sun

 7.5–10cm (3–4in)

 7–24°C (45–75°F)
Full sun, or direct light without full sun

 In winter, keep compost slightly moist; in summer, water more freely, but not excessively, ensuring the compost is well drained, and feed every 2–3 weeks with weak liquid fertilizer.

 Remove and root side-shoots in late summer and place in 15–18°C (59–64°F).

Graptopetalum paraguayense
Ghost Plant, Mother-of-pearl Plant

This succulent looks like a miniature tree clad in short stems bearing rosettes of thick, fleshy, greyish-green leaves with a silvery bloom. At first, the stems are upright, but later prostrate.

 25–30cm (10–12in)

 5–10°C (41–50°F)
Full sun

 20–25cm (8–10in)

 10–27°C (50–80°F)
Full sun, or direct light without full sun

 In winter, keep compost just moist, but not dry; in summer, water freely and feed every 2 weeks with weak liquid fertilizer.

 In spring, cut off rosettes (with several inches of stem), allow to dry slightly, then insert in well-drained compost and place in 15–18°C (59–64°F).

Haworthia margaritifera
Pearl Haworthia, Pearl Plant

Earlier known as *Haworthia pumila*, this succulent forms a stemless rosette of curved, fleshy, dark-green leaves with white, wart-like protuberances. In mid- and late summer, it develops small, bell-like, greenish-white flowers at the ends of long, wiry stems.

 7.5–10cm (3–4in)

 5–10°C (41–50°F); avoid low temperatures
Full sun

 13–15cm (5–6in)

 10–21°C (50–70°F)
Full sun, or direct light without full sun

 In winter, keep compost barely moist, especially if temperature is low; in summer, keep compost moist but allow it to dry out between waterings, and feed every 2 weeks with weak liquid fertilizer.

 Remove offsets in early summer, allow to dry slightly, pot up into well-drained compost and place in 15–18°C (59–64°F).

Kalanchoe daigremontiana
Devil's Backbone

Earlier known as *Bryophyllum daigremontianum*, this distinctive succulent has an unbranched central stem and fleshy, slightly triangular, green leaves about 10–15cm (4–6in) long. They are marbled with brown and slightly curled upward at their edges. The undersides are blotched with purple, and small plantlets develop along their edges.

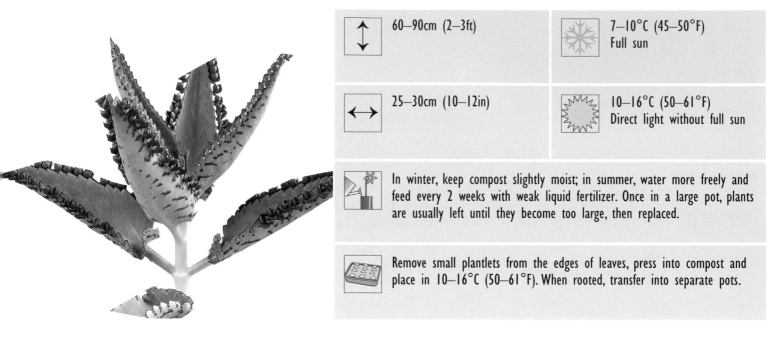

↕	60–90cm (2–3ft)	❄	7–10°C (45–50°F) Full sun
↔	25–30cm (10–12in)	☀	10–16°C (50–61°F) Direct light without full sun

In winter, keep compost slightly moist; in summer, water more freely and feed every 2 weeks with weak liquid fertilizer. Once in a large pot, plants are usually left until they become too large, then replaced.

Remove small plantlets from the edges of leaves, press into compost and place in 10–16°C (50–61°F). When rooted, transfer into separate pots.

Kalanchoe delagoensis
Chandelier Plant

Still popularly known as *Bryophyllum tubiflorum* and *Kalanchoe tubiflora*, this succulent, shrublet-like plant develops a stiff stem. The cylindrical leaves are green, blotched brown and about 7.5cm (3in) long, with a distinctive furrow. Small plantlets develop at the ends of these leaves. In spring, small, bell-shaped, orange flowers are sometimes produced.

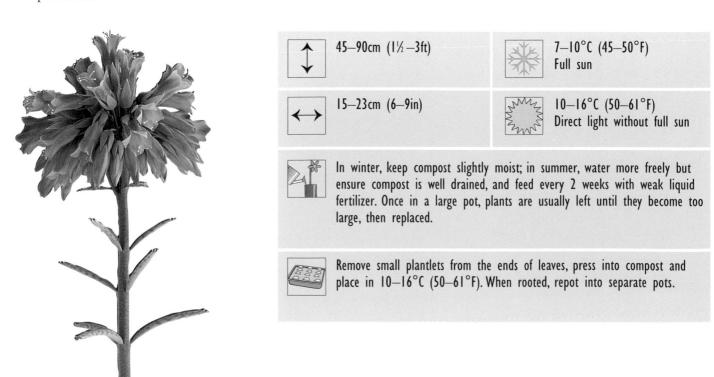

↕	45–90cm (1½–3ft)	❄	7–10°C (45–50°F) Full sun
↔	15–23cm (6–9in)	☀	10–16°C (50–61°F) Direct light without full sun

In winter, keep compost slightly moist; in summer, water more freely but ensure compost is well drained, and feed every 2 weeks with weak liquid fertilizer. Once in a large pot, plants are usually left until they become too large, then replaced.

Remove small plantlets from the ends of leaves, press into compost and place in 10–16°C (50–61°F). When rooted, repot into separate pots.

Kalanchoe tomentosa
Panda Bear Plant, Panda Plant, Plush Plant, Pussy Ears
This succulent has a mass of thick leaves, which, like the stems, are smothered with whitish hairs that create the impression of soft felt. The edges of the leaves become brown, especially towards their tips.

 30–45cm (12–18in)

 10–13°C (50–55°F)
Direct light without full sun

 20–25cm (8–10in)

13–18°C (55–64°F)
Direct light without full sun

 In winter, keep compost slightly moist; in summer, water more freely and feed every 2 weeks with weak liquid fertilizer.

Sow seeds in spring and place in 24°C (75°F).

Lithops pseudotruncatella
Flowering Stone, Living Stone, Mimicry Plant, Stoneface
Low-growing succulent with an olive-green, rounded body and brown markings radiating from a central cleft. Yellow flowers appear in early summer. There are several popular forms.

 3cm (1¼in)

 5–10°C (41–50°F)
Full sun

 36mm (1½in); forms clumps

 10–27°C (50–80°F)
Full sun

 During winter, keep compost dry; in summer, water sparingly but do not give any water until the old leaves have shrivelled (usually in late spring). Throughout summer, feed every 2 weeks with weak liquid fertilizer.

Divide congested clumps in spring and place in 10°C (50°F).

Mammillaria bocasana
Powder Puff Cactus

Desert cactus with rounded, dark, bluish-green cushions covered with white spines and silky hairs. During mid-summer it bears bell-shaped creamy-yellow flowers, 12mm (½ in) wide.

 10–15cm (4–6in)

 5–7°C (41–45°F)
Full sun

 5cm (2in); forms a mound of rounded cushions up to 15cm (6in) wide

 10–21°C (50–70°F)
Full sun

 In winter, keep compost relatively dry; in summer, water freely, ensuring the compost is well drained, and feed every 2 weeks with weak liquid fertilizer.

 Remove offsets in early summer, allow cut ends to dry slightly, insert in sandy compost and place in 10–16°C (50–61°F).

Mammillaria zeilmanniana
Rose Pincushion Cactus

This desert cactus has a cylindrical, glossy, pale-green body that forms a multiheaded clump. It is covered with tufts of fine, white hairs. During midsummer, it develops masses of reddish flowers about 18mm (¾ in) wide.

 5cm (2in)

 5–7°C (41–45°F)
Full sun

 Forms clusters

 10–21°C (50–70°F)
Full sun

 In winter, keep compost relatively dry; in summer, water freely but ensure the compost is well drained (do not let water rest on the cushions). Throughout summer, feed every 2 weeks with weak liquid fertilizer.

 Remove offsets in early summer, allow cut ends to dry slightly, insert in sandy compost and place in 10–16°C (50–61°F).

Notocactus haselbergii
Scarlet Ball Cactus

Also known as *Parodia haselbergii*, this desert cactus has a globular or cylindrical nature, with a flattened top. Its bright-green body is covered with whitish-yellow spines and 30 or more shallow, spiralling ribs. The woolly white areoles bear about 20 spines. During late spring and early summer, it produces bright orange-red flowers.

 13–15cm (5–6in)

 5–10°C (41–50°F)
Full sun

 5–7.5cm (2–3in), then spreading

 10–24°C (50–75°F)
Full sun

 In winter, keep compost dry, especially if temperature falls below the level indicated; in summer, water freely and feed every 2 weeks with weak liquid fertilizer.

 Sow seeds in spring and place in 24°C (75°F).

Notocactus leninghausii
Golden Ball Cactus

Sometimes known as *Parodia leninghausii*, this slow-growing desert cactus is initially globular, but after about 3 years has a cylindrical outline. It has a pale-green body, with about 30 ribs bearing a mixture of pale- and golden-yellow spines. From early to late summer, it produces bright yellow flowers.

 18–25cm (7–10in) in a pot, but can reach 90cm (3ft) when in a border, greenhouse or conservatory

 5–10°C (41–50°F)
Full sun

 10–13cm (4–5in)

 10–24°C (50–75°F)
Full sun

 In winter, keep compost dry, especially if temperature falls below the level indicated; in summer, water freely and feed every 2 weeks with weak liquid fertilizer.

 Sow seeds in spring and place in 24°C (75°F).

Notocactus mammulosus

Also known as *Parodia mammulosa*, this easily grown desert cactus has a globular, dark-green body that is depressed and spineless at the top. It reveals 18–20 deeply notched ribs, with yellow-brown and brown-tipped spines. During most of summer, it has yellow flowers with a red stripe on the outer petals.

↕	10cm (4in)	❄	5–10°C (41–50°F) Full sun
↔	7.5–18cm (3–7in), then spreading	☀	10–24°C (50–75°F) Full sun

In winter, keep compost dry, especially if the temperature falls below the level indicated; in summer, keep compost moist and feed every 2 weeks with weak liquid fertilizer.

Sow seeds in spring and place in 24°C (75°F).

Notocactus ottonis

Also known as *Parodia ottonis*, this desert cactus eventually has a clustering nature. Initially, it has a solitary, deep-green, cylindrical or globular body with a flattened top, about 7.5cm (3in) wide, and ribs bearing slender, yellow-brown spines. Yellow flowers, up to 10cm (4in) long, appear from late spring to midsummer.

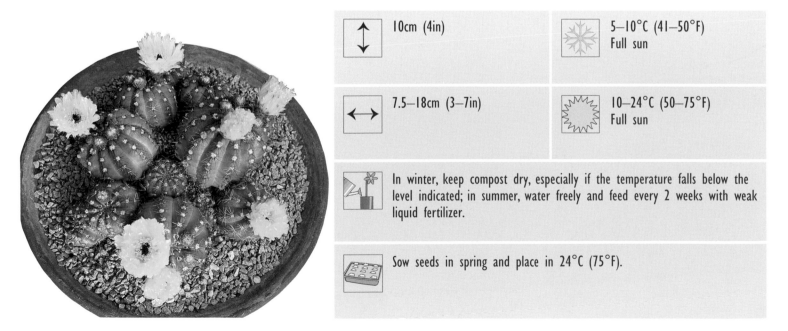

↕	10cm (4in)	❄	5–10°C (41–50°F) Full sun
↔	7.5–18cm (3–7in)	☀	10–24°C (50–75°F) Full sun

In winter, keep compost dry, especially if the temperature falls below the level indicated; in summer, water freely and feed every 2 weeks with weak liquid fertilizer.

Sow seeds in spring and place in 24°C (75°F).

Opuntia microdasys
Bunny Ears, Goldplush Plant, Prickly Pear, Rabbit's Ears, Yellow Bunny Ears
Much-branched desert cactus with bright-green, pad-like leaves that are really flattened stems. These pads do not have spines, but are covered with attractive tufts of yellow, barbed bristles. Plants in the wild develop yellow flowers, but those indoors seldom bloom. There are several superb forms with reddish or white clusters of bristles.

 25–30cm (10–12in) when grown in a pot, but up to 90cm (3ft) in a conservatory or greenhouse

 7–13°C (45–55°F); do not allow temperature to fall below the lowest figure
Full sun

 15–20cm (6–8in) when grown in a pot, but 30–38cm (12–15in) in a conservatory or greenhouse

 13–27°C (55–80°F)
Full sun

 In winter, keep compost slightly moist; in summer, water freely and feed every 2 weeks with weak liquid fertilizer.

 During midsummer, remove young pads, allow cut ends to dry, insert in sandy compost and place in 13–18°C (55–64°F).

Orbea variegata
Carrion Flower, Starfish Cactus, Toad Cactus
Also known as *Stapelia variegata*, this succulent develops grey-green stems and pale-yellow, star-like flowers in late summer and early autumn. They are 5–7.5cm (2–3in) wide, with chocolate-brown markings.

 10cm (4in)

 10°C (50°F); avoid low temperatures, which cause it to decay
Full sun

 15cm (6in), clump-forming

 10–21°C (50–70°F)
Full sun, or direct light without full sun

 In winter, keep compost slightly moist; in summer, water more freely but avoid waterlogging, and feed every 2–3 weeks with weak liquid fertilizer.

 Sow seeds in spring, in 18–21°C (64–70°C). Alternatively, divide congested clumps in spring and place in 18°C (64°F).

Pachyphytum oviferum
Moodstones, Moonstone Plant, Sugared Almond Plant
This small succulent has rounded, moisture-packed leaves that are covered in a silvery-white bloom and clustered around sturdy stems. During winter, the lower leaves tend to shrivel, especially if the temperature is low. In spring, it bears white, bell-like flowers on short stalks.

 15–20cm (6–8in)

 5–10°C (41–50°F)
Full sun

 13–15cm (5–6in)

 10–27°C (50–80°F)
Full sun

 In winter, keep compost barely moist; in summer, water more freely and feed every 2 weeks with weak liquid fertilizer.

 Where a plant has lost most of its lower leaves, cut off the top rosette of leaves, plus a piece of stem. Allow the cut surface to dry slightly, insert the stem in sandy compost and place in 15–18°C (59–64°F).

Rebutia kupperiana
Crown Cactus
Slow-growing desert cactus with a reddish-green body covered with white spines that reveal copper-coloured tips. During late spring and early summer, it develops orange-red flowers, 25–36mm (1–1½in) wide.

 36–50mm (1½–2in)

 5–10°C (41–50°F)
Full sun

 36–50mm (1½–2in); eventually forms a clump 10–13cm (4–5in) wide

 10–21°C (50–70°F)
Full sun

 In winter, keep compost barely moist; in summer, water freely but ensure good drainage, and feed every 2 weeks with weak liquid fertilizer.

 Sow seeds in spring, in 24°C (75°F).

Rebutia senilis
Crown Cactus, Fire-crown Cactus

Desert cactus with a pale-green, spherical stem depressed at its top and densely covered with silvery-white, bristly spines. During spring and midsummer, it bears funnel-shaped, carmine-red flowers, 18mm (¾in) wide, with red throats.

 7.5–10cm (3–4in)

 5–10°C (41–50°F)
Full sun

 7.5cm (3in), but eventually forms a cushion-like clump, 25–30cm (10–12in) wide

 10–21°C (50–70°F)
Direct light without full sun

 In winter, keep compost barely moist; in summer, water freely but allow the compost to dry out slightly between waterings, and feed every 2 weeks with weak liquid fertilizer.

 Sow seeds in spring and place in 24°C (75°F).

Rhipsalidopsis gaertneri
Easter Cactus

A distinctive forest cactus with many other names, including *Hatiora gaertneri*, *Epiphyllum russellianum* and *Schlumbergera gaertneri*. This may appear to be a botanist's jamboree; if in doubt, ask for the Easter Cactus. It is often confused with the Christmas Cactus (*Schlumbergera* x *buckleyi*), but usually forms a much larger plant. Its stems, although usually flat, may have 3–5 angles and notched edges. From early to late spring, it bears bright red flowers, about 6cm (2½ in) wide, with sharply pointed petals.

 38–45cm (15–18in)

 13–16°C (55–61°F)
Full sun or direct light without full sun

 75–90cm (2½–3ft)

 10–13°C (50–55°F)
In temperate climates, plants are often put outside in summer, in partial shade

 In winter, keep compost barely moist; in spring, when flower buds form, increase the amount of water and keep compost moist but not water-logged. After the flowers fade, keep compost moist but not saturated. During summer, feed every 2 weeks with weak liquid fertilizer. Repot annually after the flowers fade.

 Take cuttings during summer. Allow cut surfaces to dry, insert in equal parts moist peat and sharp sand and place in 16–18°C (61–64°F).

Schlumbergera x buckleyi
Christmas Cactus

The naming of this forest cactus is often confused and you might see it listed as *Schlumbergera hybrida*. It is a cross between *Schlumbergera russelliana* and *Schlumbergera truncata* (Crab Cactus). It is well known for its branching, flat stems with untoothed edges and joints every 5cm (2in). Its magenta or rose-coloured flowers, 5cm (2in) long and 3cm (1¼in) wide, appear from mid- to late winter.

 15–20cm (6–8in)

 13–15°C (55–59°F) Full sun, or direct light without full sun

 23–25cm (9–10in)

 In temperate climates, plants can be placed outside in partial shade; alternatively, keep at 10–13°C (50–55°F)

 In autumn, keep compost barely moist, but increase the watering frequency as soon as flower buds form. When flowering, keep compost moist, but afterwards reduce watering frequency. In summer (if the plant is outdoors), keep compost evenly moist. From when flower buds form until flowers fade, feed every 10–14 days with weak liquid fertilizer. Repot annually after flowers fade.

 Take cuttings during summer. Allow cut surfaces to dry, insert in equal parts moist peat and sharp sand and place in 16–18°C (61–64°F).

Schlumbergera truncata
Crab Cactus

Also known as *Epiphyllum truncatum* and *Zygocactus truncatus*, this forest cactus is often confused with the Christmas Cactus (*Schlumbergera x buckleyi*), which also has flattened stems. In the Crab Cactus, these flattened stems are usually 5–7.5cm (2–3in) long, with deeply incised notches along their edges. They are bright green at first, later red. From early to midwinter, it bears flowers about 5–7.5cm (2–3in) long, primarily pink to deep red, but also in shades of crimson, purple, blue and white.

 20–30cm (8–12in)

 13–15°C (55–59°F) Full sun, or direct light without full sun

 30–38cm (12–15in)

 In temperate climates, plants can be placed outside in partial shade; alternatively, keep at 10–13°C (50–55°F)

In autumn, keep compost barely moist, but increase watering as soon as flower buds form. When flowering, keep compost moist, but afterwards reduce the amount. In summer (perhaps while the plant is outdoors), keep compost evenly moist. From when flower buds form until flowers fade, feed every 10–14 days with weak liquid fertilizer. Repot annually after flowers fade.

 Take cuttings during summer. Allow cut surfaces to dry, insert in equal parts moist peat and sharp sand and place in 16–18°C (61–64°F).

Sedum morganianum
Beaver-tail, Burro's Tail, Donkey's Tail, Horse's Tail, Lamb's Tail

Succulent plant with thick, trailing stems packed with fleshy, pointed, grey-green leaves up to 18mm (¾in) long. They are covered with a whitish bloom and densely clustered towards the lower ends of the stems. From mid- to late summer, pale-pink flowers are borne in clusters at the ends of stems on large, mature plants.

	25–50mm (1–2in)		7–10°C (45–50°F); survives 5°C (41°F) for short periods if compost is kept slightly drier. Full sun
	cascading for 30–60cm (1–2ft)		10–18°C (50–64°F) Full sun, or direct light without full sun
	In winter, keep compost barely moist; in summer, water freely, allowing compost to dry out slightly between waterings, and feed every 2 weeks with weak liquid fertilizer.		
	Sow seeds in spring and place in 24°C (75°F).		

Sedum sieboldii
October Daphne, October Plant

Sometimes sold as *Hylotelephium sieboldii*, this succulent plant has long, spreading stems with rounded leaves that almost encircle them. At first, they are grey-blue, but slowly change to brownish-green with a tinge of red around the edges. Clusters of pink flowers appear at the ends of the stems in early autumn. There are several variegated forms, including 'Mediovariegatum', with slightly smaller leaves, yellow at the centre and surrounded by green.

	5–7.5cm (2–3in)		7–10°C (45–50°F); survives 5°C (41°F) for short periods if compost is kept slightly drier Full sun
	23–38cm (9–15in), then cascading		10–18°C (50–64°F) Full sun, or direct light without full sun
	In winter, keep compost barely moist; in summer, water freely, but ensure good drainage and allow compost to become slightly dry between waterings, and feed every 2 weeks with weak liquid fertilizer.		
	Divide congested plants when repotting in spring and place in 13–15°C (55–59°F).		

Senecio rowleyanus
String-of-beads

Trailing succulent plant with tough, wiry but fleshy stems that bear small, glossy-green, grape-like leaves. Sweet-scented white flowers with rich purple stigmas appear from late summer to early autumn.

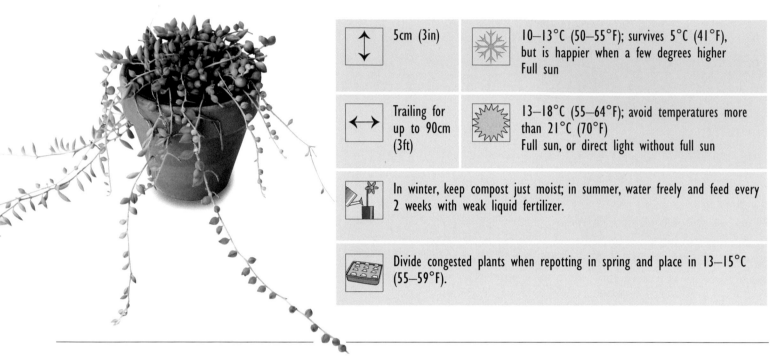

↕ 5cm (3in)	❄ 10–13°C (50–55°F); survives 5°C (41°F), but is happier when a few degrees higher. Full sun
↔ Trailing for up to 90cm (3ft)	☀ 13–18°C (55–64°F); avoid temperatures more than 21°C (70°F). Full sun, or direct light without full sun

In winter, keep compost just moist; in summer, water freely and feed every 2 weeks with weak liquid fertilizer.

Divide congested plants when repotting in spring and place in 13–15°C (55–59°F).

OTHER CACTI AND SUCCULENTS

Agave americana (American Aloe, Century Plant, Maguey): succulent with a rosette of thick, sword-shaped, saw-edged, grey-green leaves. 'Variegata', with wide yellow bands along the edges of the leaves, is usually grown indoors.

Astrophytum ornatum (Star Cactus): grey, 8-ribbed, globular body, becoming cylindrical with darker markings and bands of white scales. Stout, amber-coloured spines. Pale-yellow flowers appear in summer on mature plants.

Echeveria harmsii (Mexican Snowball, Red Echeveria): has a branching nature and lance-shaped succulent leaves that form large, loose rosettes. Clusters of scarlet, bell-shaped flowers with yellow tips in early summer.

Espostoa lanata (Snowball Cactus): eventually a large and tree-like cactus, but in cultivation usually 30cm (12in) high. Plants become covered with white, woolly hairs and spines.

Lithops optica (Flowering Stone, Living Stone, Stoneface Mimicry Plant): low-growing succulent with grey-green body and deep central cleft. Initially solitary, but later forms colonies. White, daisy-like flowers on short stems during late autumn and early winter.

Lobivia jajoiana (Cob Cactus): sometimes sold as *Echinopsis marsoneri*, this desert cactus has an almost cylindrical green body with short, pale red and black spines. Claret-coloured, short-lived flowers with black throats, 5cm (2in) wide, in summer.

Opuntia scheeri (Prickly Pear): slow-growing desert cactus. Flattened, pad-like stems are 15cm (6in) long and 5cm (2in) wide, bluish-green, somewhat oblong and covered with golden spines and yellowish-brown barbed bristles.

Pachycereus marginatus (Organ Pipe Cactus): earlier known as *Lemaireocereus marginatus*, this usually forms a column with prominent ribs packed with areoles that form a white line down the plant.

Rhipsalis baccifera (Mistletoe Cactus): also known as *Rhipsalis cassutha*, this forest cactus produces pale-green stems and round, white fruits.

PALMS AND CYCADS

Palms introduce a restful, stately aura to homes, retaining their leaves throughout the year. Some are ideal for displaying on low tables, especially when young; others are more dramatic in corners of rooms or in conservatories. Mist their leaves regularly, especially if the atmosphere is dry and the temperature high.

 HEIGHT   **SPREAD**   **WINTER**   **SUMMER**   **CARE**   **PROPAGATION**

Caryota mitis

Burmese Fishtail Palm, Clustered Fishtail Palm, Fishtail Palm, Tufted Fishtail Palm

Fishtail-type palm with ragged-edged, wedge-shaped, thick, dark-green leaflets, eventually 15cm (6in) long and 10cm (4in) wide, borne on arching stems.

1.5–2.4m (5–8ft) in a pot indoors	13–18°C (55–64°F) Full sun
60cm–1m (2–3½ ft) in a pot indoors	18–21°C (64–70°F) Direct light without full sun, or indirect light

 In winter, keep compost evenly moist; in summer, water moderately without continually saturating the compost, and feed every 3–4 weeks with weak liquid fertilizer. Repot in spring when roots fill the pot, though this vigorous palm is best restricted to a small pot. If in a large pot, do not repot but replace some of the soil with fresh compost.

 In spring, remove basal suckers, transfer to individual pots and place in 18°C (64°F).

Chamaedorea elegans
Good-luck Palm, Parlour Palm

Feather-type palm, earlier known as *Neanthe bella*, often sold when about 15cm (6in) high, in a group of palms in a large container. Later, it can be repotted into a large pot. It produces mid- to dark-green, fairly wide leaflets on **arching stems.**

 45cm–1.2m (1½–4ft)

 10–13°C (50–55°F)
Direct light without full sun

 45–75cm (1½–2½ft)

 13–18°C (55–64°F)
Indirect light or light shade

 In winter, keep compost barely moist; in summer, provide more water but ensure good drainage, and feed every 4 weeks with weak liquid fertilizer. Repot in spring only when the compost is congested – it dislikes root disturbance.

 Sow seeds in spring, place in 24–27°C (75–80°F).

Chamaedorea erumpens
Bamboo Palm

This cane-type palm has clusters of stems arising from compost level and bearing fronds with 15 deep-green leaflets.

 1.5–3m (5–10ft)

 10–13°C (50–55°F)
Direct light without full sun, or indirect light

 75cm–1.2m (2½–4ft)

 13–18°C (55–64°F)
Indirect light or light shade

 In winter, keep compost barely moist; in summer, provide more water but ensure good drainage, and feed every 4 weeks with weak liquid fertilizer. Repot in spring but only when the compost is congested – it dislikes root disturbance.

 Divide congested plants in spring and place in 13–15°C (55–59°F).

Chamaerops humilis

Dwarf Fan Palm, European Fan Palm, European Palm, Mediterranean Fan Palm

This fan-type palm, normally tufted but occasionally with a trunk, grows 9m (30ft) high in its native area. It develops fans of grey-green segments, forming leaves up to 45cm (1½ ft) long and 30cm (1ft) across, borne on coarse-toothed leaf stalks.

 90cm–1.5m (3–5ft)

 5–7°C (41–45°F)
Full sun

 90cm–1.5m (3–5ft)

 7–16°C (45–61°F)
Full sun, or direct light without full sun

 In winter, keep compost lightly moist; in summer, water freely but ensure it does not become waterlogged, and feed every 4 weeks with weak liquid fertilizer. Repot in spring when roots fill the pot, usually every 2–3 years.

 In spring, remove suckers from around the base, transfer to individual pots and place in 10–13°C (50–55°F).

Chrysalidocarpus lutescens

Areca Palm, Butterfly Palm, Cane Palm, Feather Palm, Golden Cane Palm, Yellow Palm

Earlier known as *Areca lutescens*, this palm develops cane-like stems and feather-like clusters of yellowish-green leaflets. The fronds, 90cm (3ft) long, are on canes that gently arch.

 1.5–3m (5–10ft)

 13–16°C (55–61°F)
Indirect light

 90cm–1.5m (3–5ft)

 16–27°C (61–80°F)
Indirect light or light shade

 In winter, keep compost slightly moist but do not allow to become dry; in summer, water freely and feed with weak liquid fertilizer every 4 weeks. Repot in spring when roots fill the pot, usually every 2–3 years. When large, replace some of the topsoil with fresh compost rather than repotting.

 Divide congested plants in spring or remove and pot up sucker-like growths and place in 16–18°C (61–64°F).

Cycas revoluta

False Palm, Japanese Fern Palm, Japanese Sago Palm, Sago Palm

This cycad (not palm) grows slowly, usually developing only one new leaf a year. These are dark green, palm-like and form a rosette that arises from a ball-like base.

 30–60cm (12–24in), sometimes more

 15–18°C (59–64°F)
Indirect light

 38–60cm (15–24in), sometimes more

 18–27°C (64–80°F)
Indirect light or light shade

 In winter, keep compost barely moist, especially if temperature is low; in summer, water freely but ensure good drainage, and feed with weak liquid fertilizer every 6 weeks. Repot in spring when roots fill the pot, usually every 3–4 years.

 Remove offsets in early summer and transfer to individual pots, or sow seed in spring and provide bottom heat of about 27°C (80°F).

Howea belmoreana

Belmore Sentry Palm, Curly Palm, Sentry Palm

Earlier known as *Howeia belmoreana* and *Kentia belmoreana*, this feather-type palm eventually forms a large, dominant feature. It develops large, graceful, arching fronds up to 30cm (1ft) wide and 45cm (1½ft) long.

 1.8–3m (6–10ft)

 10–12°C (50–54°F)
Full sun, or direct light without full sun

 1.5–2.4m (5–8ft)

 15–21°C (59–70°F)
Indirect light or light shade

 In winter, keep compost barely moist; in summer, water freely but ensure good drainage, and feed every 3 weeks with weak liquid fertilizer. Repot in spring when roots fill the pot, usually every 2–3 years.

 Sow seeds in spring; place in 27°C (80°F).

Howea forsteriana
Kentia Palm, Paradise Palm, Sentry Palm, Thatch Leaf Palm, Thatch Palm

Earlier known as *Howeia forsteriana* and *Kentia forsteriana*, this feather-type palm has large, wide, deep-green leaflets. It grows more rapidly than *Howea belmoreana* and its stems are less arching.

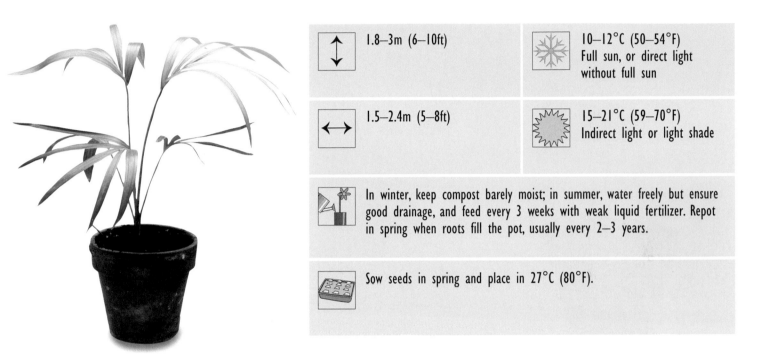

↕	1.8–3m (6–10ft)	❄	10–12°C (50–54°F) Full sun, or direct light without full sun
↔	1.5–2.4m (5–8ft)	☀	15–21°C (59–70°F) Indirect light or light shade

In winter, keep compost barely moist; in summer, water freely but ensure good drainage, and feed every 3 weeks with weak liquid fertilizer. Repot in spring when roots fill the pot, usually every 2–3 years.

Sow seeds in spring and place in 27°C (80°F).

Livistona chinensis
Chinese Fan Palm, Chinese Fountain Palm, Fan Palm

This fan-type palm has a slow-growing nature when indoors, forming large, bright-green, segmented fans with drooping tips.

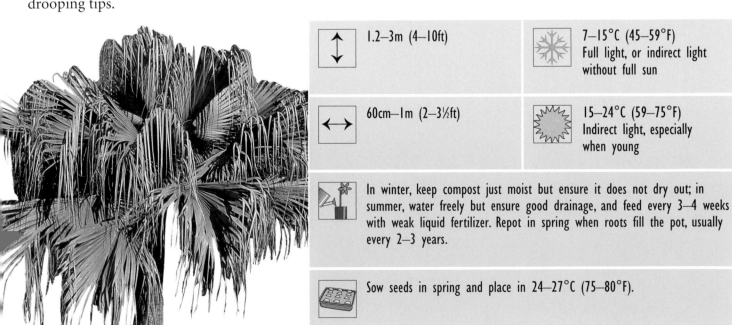

↕	1.2–3m (4–10ft)	❄	7–15°C (45–59°F) Full light, or indirect light without full sun
↔	60cm–1m (2–3½ft)	☀	15–24°C (59–75°F) Indirect light, especially when young

In winter, keep compost just moist but ensure it does not dry out; in summer, water freely but ensure good drainage, and feed every 3–4 weeks with weak liquid fertilizer. Repot in spring when roots fill the pot, usually every 2–3 years.

Sow seeds in spring and place in 24–27°C (75–80°F).

Lytocaryum weddellianum
Dwarf Coconut Palm, Weddel Palm

Earlier known as *Microcoelum weddellianum*, *Syagrus weddelliana* and *Cocos weddelliana*, this feather-type palm has a diminutive nature, only reaching 1.5–1.8m (5–6ft) high, even after 15 years. It is claimed to be one of the prettiest palms, with slightly arching fronds bearing narrow, mid- to dark-green leaflets

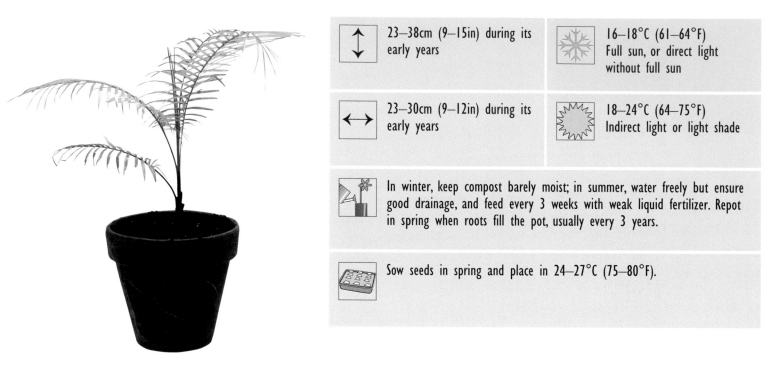

23–38cm (9–15in) during its early years

23–30cm (9–12in) during its early years

16–18°C (61–64°F)
Full sun, or direct light without full sun

18–24°C (64–75°F)
Indirect light or light shade

In winter, keep compost barely moist; in summer, water freely but ensure good drainage, and feed every 3 weeks with weak liquid fertilizer. Repot in spring when roots fill the pot, usually every 3 years.

Sow seeds in spring and place in 24–27°C (75–80°F).

Phoenix canariensis
Canary Date Palm, Canary Island Date, Canary Palm

This feather-type palm has arching stems bearing stiff, straight, narrow leaflets.

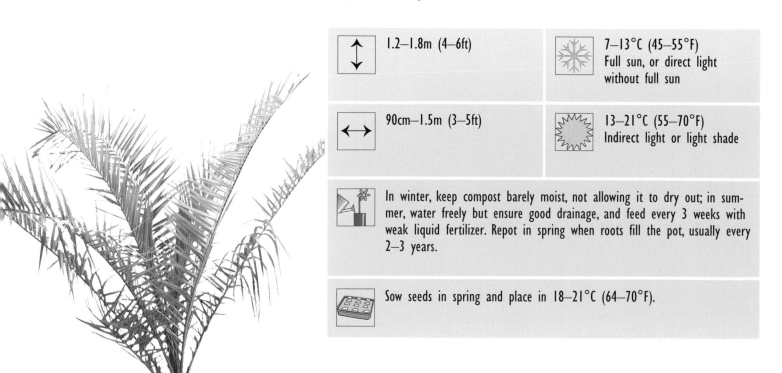

1.2–1.8m (4–6ft)

90cm–1.5m (3–5ft)

7–13°C (45–55°F)
Full sun, or direct light without full sun

13–21°C (55–70°F)
Indirect light or light shade

In winter, keep compost barely moist, not allowing it to dry out; in summer, water freely but ensure good drainage, and feed every 3 weeks with weak liquid fertilizer. Repot in spring when roots fill the pot, usually every 2–3 years.

Sow seeds in spring and place in 18–21°C (64–70°F).

Phoenix roebelenii
Miniature Date Palm, Pygmy Date Palm, Roebelin Palm

This almost stemless feather-type palm has dark-green leaves formed of many narrow leaflets. These create a crown of arching fronds that hang down at their tips.

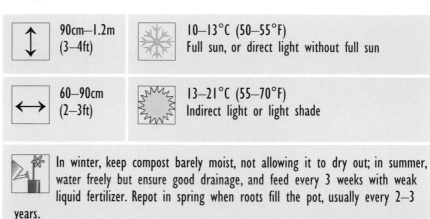

↕ 90cm–1.2m (3–4ft)	❄ 10–13°C (50–55°F) Full sun, or direct light without full sun
↔ 60–90cm (2–3ft)	☀ 13–21°C (55–70°F) Indirect light or light shade

In winter, keep compost barely moist, not allowing it to dry out; in summer, water freely but ensure good drainage, and feed every 3 weeks with weak liquid fertilizer. Repot in spring when roots fill the pot, usually every 2–3 years.

Sow seeds in spring and place in 18–21°C (64–70°F).

Rhapis excelsa
Bamboo Palm, Broad-leaved Lady Palm, Fern Rhapis, Ground Rattan, Little Lady Palm, Miniature Fan Palm

Clump-forming, fan-type palm with bamboo-like stems and mid- to dark-green, finger-like leaves radiating from their tops like a fan. Each leaf is about 20cm (8in) long.

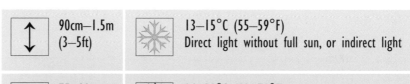

↕ 90cm–1.5m (3–5ft)	❄ 13–15°C (55–59°F) Direct light without full sun, or indirect light
↔ 75–90cm (2½–3ft)	☀ 16–21°C (61–70°F) Indirect light or light shade

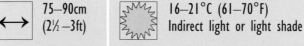

In winter, keep compost just moist; in summer, water freely but ensure good drainage, and feed with weak liquid fertilizer every 3 weeks. Repot in spring when roots fill the pot, usually every 2–3 years.

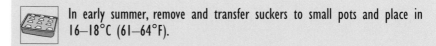

In early summer, remove and transfer suckers to small pots and place in 16–18°C (61–64°F).

OTHER INDOOR PALMS

Caryota urens (Wine Fishtail Palm): triangular leaflets on a palm with a sparse nature.

Chamaedorea seifrizii (Reed Palm): cane-type palm with deep-green, narrow leaflets.

Cocos nucifera (Coconut Palm): young plants with several leaflets often sold growing in a pot, with a coconut at the base.

Washingtonia filifera (Californian Fan Palm): fast-growing palm, eventually forming a dominant feature.

It is usually short-lived indoors when grown as a potplant, but is well worth growing, with brilliant green leaves displayed in large fans.

Washingtonia robusta (Mexican Fan Palm, Thread Palm): fan-like, with deep-green leaves.

BULBS

Bulbs, such as daffodils, tulips and hyacinths, are nature's powerhouses of stored energy. They are formed of fleshy leaves arising from a basal plate and tightly wrapped around each other. Although botanically different, corms, tubers and rhizomes are often grouped with bulbs. Corms are swollen stem bases (crocuses, freesias, sparaxis), tubers are swollen roots or stems (dahlias), and rhizomes are horizontal stems, either wholly underground or partly above, (Lily-of-the-valley, Bearded Irises).

 HEIGHT   **SPREAD**   **WINTER**   **SUMMER**   **CARE**   **PROPAGATION**

Freesia hybrids
Freesia, Florist's Freesia

These cormous hybrids are usually grown for flowering indoors from midwinter to spring. They have fragrant, funnel-shaped flowers in a wide colour range, including white, yellow, blue, orange, pink and red.

	45cm (1½ft)		*See below*
	20–25cm (8–10in), when five corms are planted in a pot 13cm (5in) wide		*See below*

From late summer to late autumn, plant 5 corms in a pot 13cm (5in) wide, using loam-based compost. Just cover the tops of the corms and sprinkle a 25mm (1in) layer of fine peat over the top. Initially, place in 5°C (41°F), keeping compost lightly moist. From mid-autumn, increase the amount of water; as growth begins, slowly raise the temperature to 13°C (55°F) and increase the amount of direct light. Keep compost moist while flowering; when flowers fade, reduce the amount of water and lower the temperature to 5°C (41°F). Allow the corms and compost to become completely dry. In late summer, remove the corms, store in a dry, frost-proof shed and plant outdoors the following spring.

 Use fresh corms each year for flowering indoors. Plants can also be raised from seeds sown in spring in 16°C (61°F). Before sowing, soak seed in clean water for 24 hours. Germination takes up to 3 weeks.

Hippeastrum **hybrids**
Amaryllis

This widely grown bulbous plant should not be confused with *Amaryllis belladonna* (Belladonna Lily), a popular bulbous autumn-flowering plant grown outdoors in warm and temperate climates. Hippeastrums mainly flower in winter and spring, but with careful timing can flower any time of year. They have green, strap-like leaves and stiff, upright stems with 3–4 funnel-shaped flowers, 7.5cm (3in) wide, in a range of single and mixed colours.

 30–38cm (12–15in)

 13–16°C (55–61°F)
Bright, indirect light when flowering

 20–25cm (8–10in)

 13–16°C (55–61°F)
Bright, indirect light when flowering

 Plant one bulb in a 13cm (5in) wide pot, leaving half the bulb exposed. Give only a little water until growth begins, then water more freely and feed every 10 days with weak liquid fertilizer.
- Bulbs of winter- and spring-flowering types are potted in early and mid-autumn.
- Specially prepared bulbs for flowering in early winter are planted in late autumn.
- For flowering during summer and early autumn, plant in early spring.

 Buy fresh bulbs each year. Alternatively, old bulbs can be restarted into growth. Gradually reduce the amount of water after plants flower and leaves turn yellow. Then, withhold water and allow compost to dry. Place in 5–7°C (41–45°F) until restarting into growth the following season.

Hyacinthus orientalis
Common Hyacinth, Dutch Hyacinth

This popular bulbous plant flowers during winter until early spring. The candle-like heads are packed with scented, wax-like flowers in a wide colour range – white, yellow, pink, red, mauve and blue.

 15–23cm (6–9in)

 When shoot tips appear above the compost's surface, place in 10°C (50°F); gradually increase to 18°C (64°F) when the flower buds show colour
Direct light without full sun

 7.5–13cm (3–5in)

 Not applicable

 Usually, pots or bowls of hyacinths are bought when buds are just starting to show colour. Keep compost evenly moist, increasing the amount of water as foliage and flowers develop. No feeding or repotting is necessary.

 After flowers fade, place the pot and plants in 5–7°C (41–45°F) in a vermin-proof shed. Later, plant into a garden.

Lachenalia aloides
Cape Cowslip

Earlier known as *Lachenalia tricolor*, this bulbous plant has strap-like leaves that arch slightly at their tips. They are pale green, about 23cm (9in) long, flecked and spotted in pale purple. Nodding, tubular, bell-shaped yellow flowers with red markings and green edges appear from midwinter to early spring. Varieties include 'Aurea' (orange-yellow).

	23–30cm (9–12in)		7–13°C (41–55°F) when in flower; avoid high temperatures Direct light without full sun
	23cm (9in)		Not applicable

 Keep compost evenly moist while flowering and continue until after the foliage dies. Keep compost dry until late summer, then repot into a clean pot and fresh compost.

 Although plants can be kept from season to season, fresh plants are usually bought each year.

Lilium longiflorum
Easter Lily, White Trumpet Lily

This bulbous plant is widely grown as a houseplant. During mid- and late summer, it produces heavily fragrant, trumpet-shaped, white flowers with golden pollen, 13–18cm (5–7in) long and 13cm (5in) across. Several other lilies are grown indoors, including *Lilium auratum* (Golden-rayed Lily), *Lilium speciosum* (Japanese Lily) and Mid-century hybrids.

	75–90cm (2½–3ft)		*See* below
	20–25cm (8–10in)		*See* below

 As soon as bulbs are available in autumn, pot them singly into 15–20cm (6–8in) pots, using soil-based compost. Cover the bulb's top with 36–50mm (1½–2in) of compost. Water the compost and place in a dark position with a temperature of about 3–5°C (37–41°F) to encourage root development. Keep compost lightly moist. When new shoots appear, move into light shade; gradually increase light and raise the temperature to 8–10°C (46–50°F) — no higher. When flowers fade, reduce to 3–5°C (37–41°F) and keep compost moist to prevent bulbs drying out.

Buy fresh bulbs each year. After flowering, place the pot in a cool, shaded position outdoors. Plant bulbs into a border early the following spring.

Narcissus
Daffodil

Many types of daffodils can be encouraged to flower indoors; most popular is the large-trumpet type with one flower on each stem. Suitable varieties include 'Dutch Master' (yellow), 'King Alfred' (yellow) and 'Spellbinder' (yellow and white). Bulbs specially prepared by nurserymen for early flowering are essential.

 38–45cm (15–18in)

 See below

 30cm (12in) when several bulbs are planted in a pot 18–23cm (7–9in) wide

 See below

 In late summer, select a pot 18–23cm (7–9in) wide and half fill it with damp bulb-fibre or potting compost. Place bulbs close together on top, noses level with the container's rim. Pack and firm further bulb-fibre or compost around each bulb, so the surface is 12mm (½ in) below the pot's rim. Thoroughly water the potting mixture, put the pot in a black polythene bag and place in a cool shed, i.e. 3–5°C (37–41°F). Regularly check compost is moist. Leave bulbs in the bag for 12–15 weeks, until shoots are 10cm (4in) high. Remove the bag and take bulbs indoors, slowly increasing temperature from 7°C (45°F) to 15°C (59°F). Keep compost moist.

Buy fresh bulbs each year.

Sparaxis tricolor
Harlequin Flower

Half-hardy in temperate climates, this cormous plant is ideal for growing indoors. Mainly the hybrids are grown. The wide colour range includes shades of red, yellow and purple, white and multicolours. Flowering is during late spring and early summer, with several star-shaped, flat-faced, 6-petalled flowers, about 36mm (1½ in) wide, on each stem.

 30–38cm (12–15in)

 See below

 20–25cm (8–10in)

 See below

 In late summer or early autumn, plant 5 corms in a pot 13cm (5in) wide, using loam-based compost. Water the compost and place the pot in 3–5°C (37–41°F). In late winter or early spring, as growth begins, provide more water and gradually move the pot into 7–10°C (45–50°F), no higher. After flowering, allow compost to dry slightly.

 Use fresh corms each year; old ones can be planted into a warm, wind-sheltered border outdoors.

Tulipa
Tulips

Tulips such as 'Single Early' and 'Double Early' types are suitable for forcing into early flower in spring indoors. 'Single Early' types have flowers, 7.5–13cm (3–5in) wide, usually with pointed buds and flowers that open flat. 'Double Early' types have flowers up to 10cm (4in) wide that resemble double-flowered paeonies. The range of varieties and colours is wide, including pink, yellow, orange, red and mixed colours. Always use specially prepared bulbs when forcing tulips into early flower.

 23–38cm (9–15in), depending on variety

 See below

 23cm (9in) when several bulbs are planted in a pot 18–23cm (7–9in) wide

 See below

 As soon as bulbs are available in late summer, select a pot 18–23cm (7–9in) wide. Fill the base with damp bulb-fibre or potting compost and place bulbs close together (but not touching) on top of it. Their noses should be below the surface of the potting mixture, which in turn is 12mm (½in) below the container's rim. Pack and firm compost around the bulbs, then water. Put the pot in a black polythene bag and place in a cool shed, i.e. 3–5°C (37–41°F). Some 14–16 weeks later (less for specially prepared bulbs) shoots will be about 5cm (2in) high. Remove the black bag and place the pot in 45–50°C (7–10°F). Later, when the foliage is 10cm (4in) high, increase the temperature to 18°C (64°F). Throughout, keep compost moist but not waterlogged.

 Buy fresh bulbs each year.

Vallota speciosa
Scarborough Lily

Sometimes known as *Cyrtanthus elatus*, this is ideal for growing on sunny window ledges indoors. From midsummer to early autumn the evergreen plants produce heads packed with up to 10 bright scarlet, funnel-shaped flowers, each about 7.5cm (3in) long.

 38–45cm (15–18in)

 25cm (10in)

 See below

 See below

 Pot up small bulbs in 7.5cm (3in) pots; larger bulbs, up to 7.5cm (3in) wide, in 13cm (5in) wide pots. Pot up in early autumn (although spring is also possible); leave the top of each bulb protruding 12–18mm (½–¾in) above the compost, lightly water and place in 3–5°C (37–41°F). Initially, place in light shade; as growth begins, gradually increase the amount of light to direct light but not full sun. In spring, slowly increase temperature to 10°C (50°F), water more freely and place in direct light without full sun. In summer, place on a warm, sunny windowsill and keep compost moist.

 Remove offsets in autumn or spring and pot up into small pots. Offsets take up to 3 years to reach flowering size, until which time place in a greenhouse that is frost-free in winter and gently warm in summer.

Veltheimia capensis
Forest Lily

This bulbous plant has shiny, mid- to dark-green, wavy-edged leaves about 23cm (9in) long. Their ends curl downwards. In spring, a tall stem, 23cm (9in) or more high, bears a tapering flower head measuring about 10cm (4in). These are packed with small, bell-shaped, pale-pink flowers with greenish tips. Varieties exist in other colours.

 25–30cm (10–12in), sometimes slightly more *See below*

 20–25cm (8–10in) *See below*

 In early autumn, plant a bulb in a pot 7.5–13cm (3–5in) wide, using soil-based, well-drained compost. Leave the top of the bulb about 6mm (¼in) above the compost's surface. Water the compost and place in 3–5°C (37–41°F) in light shade. Increase watering frequency once growth begins, and raise the temperature to 10–13°C (50–55°F). Position the pot in slightly stronger sunlight and keep compost moist. After flowering, allow the foliage to die back. Rest the plant; in autumn repot the bulb into fresh compost.

 Remove offset bulbs from mature bulbs in autumn, transfer to small pots and place in 3–5°C (37–41°F). Sometimes, small bulbs are left around the main bulb to produce a larger plant.

OTHER BULBOUS PLANTS

Eucomis comosa (Pineapple Lily): rosette-forming basal leaves and long, poker-like head packed with green flowers in late summer.

Ixia hybrids (African Corn Lily): star-shaped, 6-petalled flowers, 5cm (2in) wide, with dark centres amid narrow, sword-like leaves during early summer. Range of colours.

Ornithogalum thyrsoides (Chincherinchee): erect, somewhat cone-shaped flower heads packed with fragrant white, cream or yellow flowers, 25mm (1in) wide, during early and midsummer.

Polianthes tuberosa (Tuberose): tall stems bearing lax heads of fragrant pure-white flowers, 25mm (1in) wide, during summer.

Eucomis comosa.

BROMELIADS AND AIR-PLANTS

Bromeliads are a diverse group of plants; some grow at ground level, while others known as air-plants are at home in trees. Some have attractive foliage, others spectacular flowers. A few have both qualities. Many have 'urns' at their centres, through which they can be watered and fed. Remember to tip out old water and replenish with fresh water every 3–4 weeks. Mist regularly as they enjoy a humid atmosphere.

 HEIGHT   **SPREAD**   **WINTER**   **SUMMER**   **CARE**   **PROPAGATION**

Aechmea chantinii
Amazonian Zebra Plant, Urn Plant

This has a rosette of spine-edged and tipped green leaves, 30–38cm (12–15in) long and 5–6cm (2–2½ in) wide. Leaves are cross-banded in silver-grey on both sides. During late summer and into autumn, orange to bright-red flowers develop.

45–75cm (1½–2½ ft)	13–18°C (55–64°F) Indirect light
38–45cm (15–18in)	18–27°C (64–80°F) Indirect light or light shade

 In winter, keep compost just moist and the urn full of water; in summer, water more freely, keeping the urn full of water. From late spring to late summer, feed every 4 weeks with weak liquid fertilizer applied to the compost and in the urn.

 Once a plant has flowered, the urn slowly dies and growth is taken over by offsets growing around it. Cut off the main plant at compost level. Once offsets are ⅓–½ the size of a full-grown parent plant, sever one close to its base with a sharp knife. Allow the cut surface to dry for 1–2 days then pot up into a clean pot with well-drained compost. Use a thin stake for support if necessary. Place in 18–21°C (64–70°F).

Aechmea fasciata
Silvery Vase, Urn Plant, Vase Plant

Greyish-green leaves cross-banded in silvery-white, up to 50cm (20in) long and 6cm (2½ in) wide, form an urn. During late summer and into autumn, a stem emerges from the urn and produces a flower head up to 15cm (6in) long. The pale-blue flowers turn rose-coloured.

 38–45cm (15–18in)

 13–15°C (55–59°F)
Indirect light

 38–50cm (15–20in)

 15–24°C (59–75°F)
Indirect light to light shade

 In winter, keep compost just moist and the urn full of water; in summer, water more freely, keeping the urn full of water. Feed every 4 weeks from late spring to late summer with weak fertilizer applied to the compost and in the urn.

 Once a plant has flowered, the rosette slowly dies and growth is taken over by offsets growing around it. Cut off the main plant at compost level. Once offsets are ⅓–½ the size of a full-grown parent plant, sever one close to its base with a sharp knife. Allow the cut surface to dry for 1–2 days then pot up into a clean pot with well-drained compost. Use a thin stake for support if necessary. Place in 18–21°C (64–70°F).

Aechmea **Foster s Favourite**
Lacquered Wine Cup

This relatively small aechmea, with sparse, tapering, deep wine-red leaves forming a central urn, develops a flower spike of coral petals tipped blue in late summer.

 30–38cm (12–15in)

 13–15°C (55–59°F)
Indirect light

 30–45cm (12–18in)

 15–24°C (59–75°F)
Indirect light to light shade

 In winter, keep compost just moist and the urn full of water; in summer, water more freely, keeping the urn full of water. Feed every 4 weeks from late spring to late summer with weak liquid fertilizer applied to the compost and in the urn.

 Once a plant has flowered, the rosette slowly dies and growth is taken over by offsets growing around it. Cut off the main plant at compost level. Once offsets are ⅓–½ the size of a full-grown parent plant, sever pnr close to its base with a sharp knife. Allow the cut surface to dry for 1–2 days then pot up into a clean pot with well-drained compost. Use a thin stake for support if necessary. Place in 18–21°C (64–70°F).

Aechmea fulgens
Coral Berry, Urn Plant

Broad, strap-like, finely spine-edged, olive-green leaves with waxy-grey undersides form a wide rosette. With age, leaves become greyish. Purplish-blue flowers appear in late summer and early autumn, followed by long-lasting, bright scarlet berries. The form 'Discolor' has leaves with purple undersides and white, powdery scales.

 25–38cm (10–15in)   30–38cm (12–15in)   13–15°C (55–59°F) Indirect light

 In winter, keep compost just moist and the urn full of water; in summer, water freely, keeping the urn full of water. Feed every 4 weeks from late spring to late summer with weak fertilizer applied to the compost and in the urn.

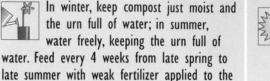 15–24°C (59–75°F) Indirect light or light shade

Once a plant has flowered, the rosette slowly dies and growth is taken over by offsets growing around it. Cut off the main plant at compost level. Once offsets are ⅓–½ the size of a full-grown parent plant, sever one close to its base with a sharp knife. Allow the cut surface to dry for 1–2 days then pot up into a clean pot with well-drained compost, using a thin stake for support if necessary. Place in 18–21°C (64–70°F).

Ananas comosus
Common Pineapple, Edible Pineapple

Earlier known as *Ananas sativus*, this member of the Pineapple family grows 1.2m (4ft) or more high, but is usually half this height when indoors. It forms a rosette of arching, pointed, strap-like, grey-green leaves that become tinged red if in strong sunlight. The short flower stem produces blue-petalled flowers with small pink bracts. Fruits appear about 6 months after the flowers, though seldom on plants indoors. *Ananas comosus* var. *variegatus* (Variegated Pineapple), which is pictured below, is smaller, with leaves variegated green, white, yellow and pink.

 45–75cm (1½–2½ ft)   13–24°C (55–75°F) Full sun

 60–75cm (2–2½ ft)   15–24°C (59–75°F) Direct light without full sun

 In winter, keep compost just moist and increase watering frequency as the plant becomes more active, allowing compost to dry out slightly between each application. Throughout summer, feed every 4 weeks with weak liquid fertilizer. Repot plants in spring, usually every other year.

 During spring, sever offsets from around the base, allow cut ends to dry for a day, then transfer to compost in a pot. Place in 21°C (70°F).

Ananas bracteatus
Red Pineapple, Wild Pineapple

Also known as *Ananas sagenaria*, this slow-growing pineapple forms a rosette of leaves similar to *Ananas comosus*. It has lavender-coloured flowers, followed by brownish fruits. *Ananas bracteatus striatus* (also known as *tricolor*) has leaves brightly coloured in green, cream and pink stripes.

 60–75cm (2–2½ ft)

 13–24°C (55–75°F)
Full sun

 60–75cm (2–2½ ft)

 15–24°C (59–75°F)
Direct light without full sun

 In winter, keep compost just moist and increase watering frequency as the plant becomes more active, allowing compost to dry out slightly between each application Throughout summer, feed every 4 weeks with weak liquid fertilizer. Repot in spring, usually every other year.

 During spring, sever offsets from around the plant's base and allow cut ends to dry for a day, then transfer them to compost in a pot. Place in 21°C (70°F).

Billbergia nutans
Angel's Tears, Friendship Plant, Queen's Tears

Narrow, dark-green leaves and arching stems bear large pink bracts and long, tubular green flowers edged in blue, with golden-yellow stamens.

 38–50cm (15–20in)

 10–13°C (50–55°F)
Full sun

 30–45cm (12–18in)

 16–24°C (61–75°F)
Indirect light without full sun

 In winter, allow compost to become almost dry before applying further water; in summer, water more freely and feed every 3–4 weeks with weak liquid fertilizer. Repot in spring when roots fill the pot.

 During spring, remove offsets, transfer to individual pots and place in 18–21°C (64–70°F).

Cryptanthus acaulis
Green Earth Star, Starfish Plant

This stemless bromeliad has wavy, tooth-edged, pale- to mid-green leaves that form a low rosette. Three-petalled, scented, rather insignificant white flowers appear at any time of year, but it is invariably grown for its attractive leaves. The larger form *argenteus* is peppered with silvery scales, while *ruber* (sometimes 'Rubra') has a purple-brown shade over the green. *Roseo-pictus'* leaves are longitudinally striped in several colours.

 5–7.5cm (2–3in)

 16–20°C (61–68°F)
Full sun, or direct light without full sun

 7.5–13cm (3–5in)

 21–27°C (70–80°F)
Full sun, or direct light without full sun

 In winter, keep compost barely moist; in summer, water more freely, ensuring compost is well-drained, and feed every 5–6 weeks with weak liquid fertilizer. Repot in spring when roots fill the pot.

 In spring or early summer, remove offsets, transfer to individual pots and place in 18–21°C (64–70°F).

Cryptanthus bivittatus
Earth Star

Distinctive and easily grown, this rosette-forming plant has crinkle-edged, lance-shaped, light-green leaves with dark-green stripes down the centre.

 6–7.5cm (2½–3in)

 16–20°C (61–68°F)
Full sun, or direct light without full sun

 15–25cm (6–10in)

 21–27°C (70–80°F)
Full sun, or direct light without full sun

 In winter, keep compost barely moist; in summer, water more freely but ensure it is well drained, and feed every 5–6 weeks with weak liquid fertilizer. Repot in spring when roots fill the pot.

 In spring or early summer, remove offsets, transfer to individual pots and place in 18–21°C (64–70°F).

Cryptanthus bromelioides
Pink Cryptanthus

Upright, spreading plant with finely spine-edged, mid-green leaves borne on slender stalks. The form *tricolor* (known as Rainbow Star), is more colourful, with green leaves striped with creamy-white lines and flushed pale pink.

 20–30cm (8–12in)

 16–20°C (61–68°F) Full sun, or direct light without full sun

 25–38cm (10–15in)

 21–27°C (70–80°F) Full sun, or direct light without full sun

 In winter, keep compost barely moist; in summer, water more freely but ensure good drainage, and feed every 5–6 weeks with weak liquid fertilizer. Repot in early summer when roots fill the pot.

 In spring or early summer, remove offsets, transfer to individual pots and place in 18–21°C (64–70°F).

Cryptanthus fosterianus
Pheasant Leaf

This spreading, rosette-forming plant has finely spine-edged, copper-brown leaves with greyish cross-banding on the upper surface. The undersides are covered with grey scales.

 6–7.5cm (2½–3in)

 16–20°C (61–68°F) Full sun, or direct light without full sun

 20–38cm (10–15in)

 21–27°C (70–80°F) Full sun, or direct light without full sun

 In winter, keep compost barely moist; in summer, water more freely but ensure good drainage, and feed every 5–6 weeks with weak liquid fertilizer. Repot in early summer when roots fill the pot.

 In spring or early summer, remove offsets, transfer to individual pots and place in 18–21°C (64–70°F).

Cryptanthus zonatus
Zebra Plant

Green leaves form a rosette with irregular transverse bands of green and golden-brown. There are forms, including *fuscus*, with reddish-brown leaves.

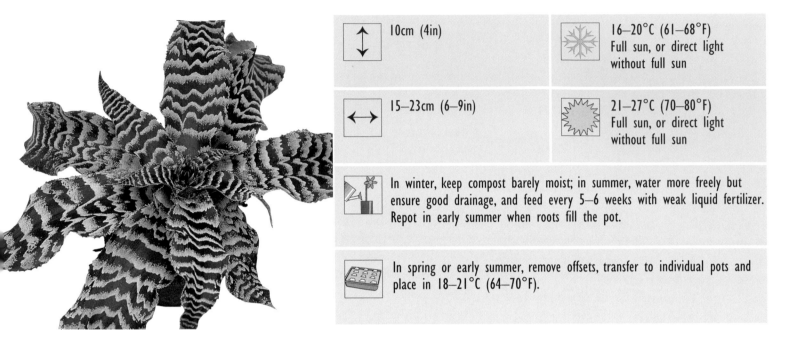

↕ 10cm (4in)	❄ 16–20°C (61–68°F) Full sun, or direct light without full sun
↔ 15–23cm (6–9in)	☀ 21–27°C (70–80°F) Full sun, or direct light without full sun

In winter, keep compost barely moist; in summer, water more freely but ensure good drainage, and feed every 5–6 weeks with weak liquid fertilizer. Repot in early summer when roots fill the pot.

In spring or early summer, remove offsets, transfer to individual pots and place in 18–21°C (64–70°F).

Guzmania lingulata
Scarlet Star

Shiny, bright metallic-green leaves form a rosette. During summer, a flowering stem arises from it, with large red bracts surrounded by small, yellowish-white flowers. These are short-lived, but the bracts remain for several weeks. *Guzmania lingulata minor*, known as Orange Star and sometimes sold as *Guzmania minor*, has bright orange-red bracts.

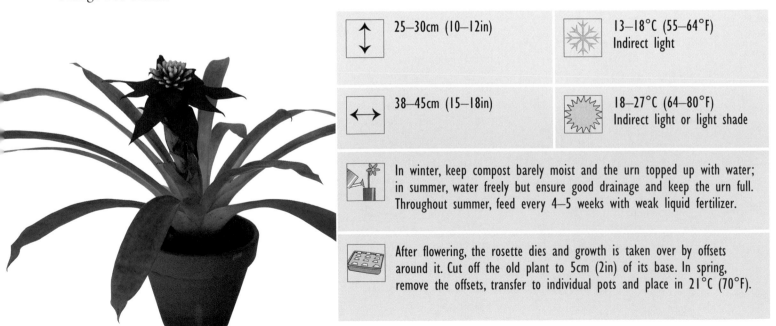

↕ 25–30cm (10–12in)	❄ 13–18°C (55–64°F) Indirect light
↔ 38–45cm (15–18in)	☀ 18–27°C (64–80°F) Indirect light or light shade

In winter, keep compost barely moist and the urn topped up with water; in summer, water freely but ensure good drainage and keep the urn full. Throughout summer, feed every 4–5 weeks with weak liquid fertilizer.

After flowering, the rosette dies and growth is taken over by offsets around it. Cut off the old plant to 5cm (2in) of its base. In spring, remove the offsets, transfer to individual pots and place in 21°C (70°F).

Guzmania monostachya
Striped Torch

Also known as *Guzmania monostachia*, this has narrow green, slightly arching leaves that form a rosette. The plant develops large, poker-like flower spikes on stems about 38cm (15in) high, with small green bracts tipped with white and vertically striped in brown and purple. Towards its top, the bracts become vermilion. Only one flower stem is produced on each plant.

 30–38cm (12–15in)

 13–18°C (55–64°F)
Indirect light

 38–60cm (15–24in)

 18–27°C (64–80°F)
Light shade

 In winter, keep compost barely moist, with the urn topped up with water; in summer, water freely, but ensure good drainage and keep the urn full. Throughout summer, feed every 4–5 weeks with weak liquid fertilizer.

 After flowering, the rosette dies and growth is taken over by offsets around it. Cut off the old plant to 5cm (2in) of its base. In spring, remove the offsets, transfer to individual pots and place in 21°C (70°F).

Neoregelia carolinae
Blushing Bromeliad

Sometimes known as *Nidularium meyendorffii*, this vase-forming bromeliad forms a wide rosette of strap-like, glossy, bright-green leaves with pointed tips. It flowers at any time of the year; flowering encourages the leaves around the rosette to turn purple or bright red. It develops small, violet-blue flowers surrounded by glossy, red bracts. There are several forms of this plant, including *tricolor*, with glossy-green leaves lined with cream and rose-pink stripes.

 23–30cm (9–12in)

 13–15°C (55–59°F)
Direct light without full sun

 38–50cm (15–20in)

 16–27°C (61–80°F)
Indirect light or light shade

 In winter, keep compost just moist and the urn full of water; in summer, water the compost moderately, also topping up the water in the urn, and feed every 5 weeks with a weak liquid fertilizer. Repot young plants in spring, usually every 3–4 years.

 In early summer, remove offsets, transfer to individual pots and place in 21°C (70°F).

Neoregelia spectabilis
Fingernail Plant

This has narrow, shiny-green leaves with crimson tips. The upper sides often have red flecks, while the undersides are ash-grey and banded. At flowering time, the centre of the plant turns rose-red, followed by a dense head of blue flowers and purple-brown bracts.

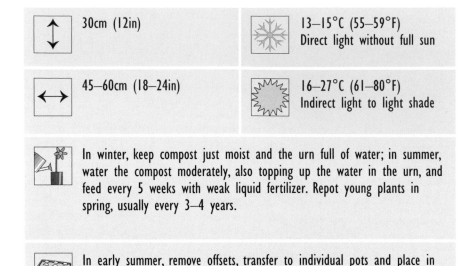

↕ 30cm (12in)	❄ 13–15°C (55–59°F) Direct light without full sun
↔ 45–60cm (18–24in)	☀ 16–27°C (61–80°F) Indirect light to light shade

In winter, keep compost just moist and the urn full of water; in summer, water the compost moderately, also topping up the water in the urn, and feed every 5 weeks with weak liquid fertilizer. Repot young plants in spring, usually every 3–4 years.

In early summer, remove offsets, transfer to individual pots and place in 21°C (70°F).

Nidularium fulgens
Blushing Bromeliad

Stemless bromeliad with shiny, light-green arching leaves that form an urn at their base. The impressive flower is formed of red bracts tipped with green, together with 3-petalled, violet-blue flowers.

↕ 25–30cm (10–12in)	❄ 13–16°C (55–61°F) Indirect light
↔ 25–30cm (10–12in)	☀ 16–24°C (61–75°F) Indirect light or light shade

In winter, keep compost barely moist and the urn filled with water; in summer, water moderately, keeping the urn filled, and feed every 4 weeks with weak liquid fertilizer. Repot in early summer.

Plants are usually short-lived; once the flowers fade, the rosette dies but the offsets continue growing. Detach them in spring, transfer to individual pots and place in 18–21°C (64–70°F).

Nidularium innocentii
Bird's Nest Bromeliad

This urn-forming bromeliad has a large rosette of finely tooth-edged, strap-like, glossy-surfaced, brownish-green leaves with metallic-purple undersides. During summer, a short stem arises from the urn, bearing 6–8 bracts surrounded by a few small, white flowers. There are several forms, including *striatum* (wide yellow stripes on the leaves and rose-red bracts) and *purpureum* (purplish-brown leaves).

 38–45cm (15–18in)

 13–16°C (55–61°F)
Indirect light

 38–45cm (15–18in)

 16–24°C (61–75°F)
Light shade

 In winter, keep compost barely moist but the urn filled with water; in summer, water moderately and keep the urn filled, and feed every 4 weeks with weak liquid fertilizer. Repot in early summer.

 Plants are usually short-lived; once the flowers fade, the rosette dies and offsets continue growing. Detach them in spring, transfer to individual pots and place in 18–21°C (64–70°F).

Tillandsia circinnata
Air-plant, Pot-bellied Tillandsia

This epiphytic tillandsia gains one of its common names from the egg-like swelling (a pseudobulb) at its base. Grey leaf blades, up to 20cm (8in) long, are usually twisted, curled or in spirals. The plant bears blue flowers with pink bracts.

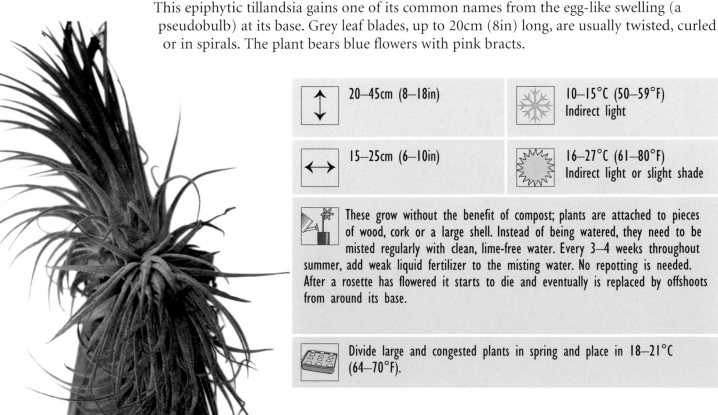

 20–45cm (8–18in)

 10–15°C (50–59°F)
Indirect light

15–25cm (6–10in)

16–27°C (61–80°F)
Indirect light or slight shade

 These grow without the benefit of compost; plants are attached to pieces of wood, cork or a large shell. Instead of being watered, they need to be misted regularly with clean, lime-free water. Every 3–4 weeks throughout summer, add weak liquid fertilizer to the misting water. No repotting is needed. After a rosette has flowered it starts to die and eventually is replaced by offshoots from around its base.

 Divide large and congested plants in spring and place in 18–21°C (64–70°F).

Other epiphytic tillandsias

Tillandsia argentea: narrow leaves smothered in silvery-grey scales; red or green bracts and bright red petals.

Tillandsia caput-medusae: bulbous base; narrow leaves clothed in white scales; flowers formed of red, pink and green bracts, and violet petals.

Tillandsia ionantha (Blushing Bride): stemless rosettes formed of silvery-grey, scale-like leaves. In summer, just before violet-purple flowers with yellow stamens appear, the centres of the leafy rosettes become flushed red.

Tillandsia usneoides (Spanish Moss, Old Man's Beard, Grey Beard): Often forms pendulous clusters up to 1m (3½ ft) long from telegraph poles in its native southeast states of the USA. Tangled, wiry stems with scaly, silvery-grey leaves; bright, yellow-green flowers in summer.

Tillandsia usneoides

Tillandsia cyanea
Pink Quill

This tillandsia is grown in a pot rather than attached to a piece of wood or bark. The narrow green leaves, about 38cm (15in) long and 25mm (1in) wide, are reddish-brown at the base. During late summer, a short, central stem develops, producing a flower head of rose to red bracts, tinged green, and violet-blue flowers.

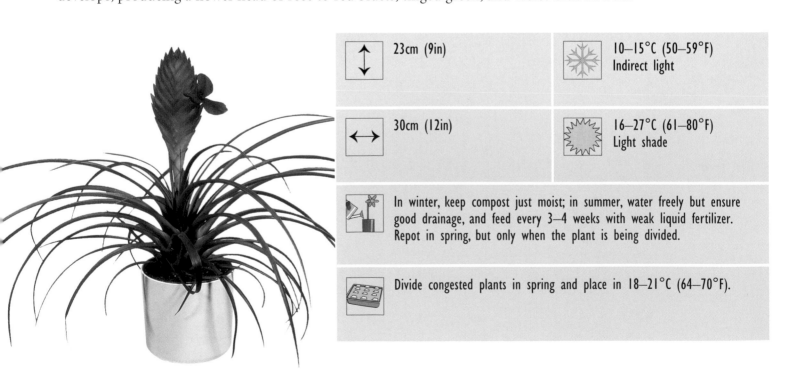

↕	23cm (9in)	❄	10–15°C (50–59°F) Indirect light
↔	30cm (12in)	☀	16–27°C (61–80°F) Light shade

In winter, keep compost just moist; in summer, water freely but ensure good drainage, and feed every 3–4 weeks with weak liquid fertilizer. Repot in spring, but only when the plant is being divided.

Divide congested plants in spring and place in 18–21°C (64–70°F).

Tillandsia lindenii
Blue-flowered Torch
Grown in a pot, it has dark-green, grass-like leaves, 30cm (12in) long. They arch outward and are purple on their undersides. During summer, a short, flattened head is produced, 15–20cm (6–8in) long, with pink bracts and white-throated blue flowers.

 38–50cm (15–20in)

 13–15°C (55–59°F)
Direct light without full sun

 30–38cm (12–15in)

 16–27°C (61–80°F)
Indirect light to light shade

 In winter, keep compost just moist; in summer, water the compost moderately and feed every 5 weeks with weak liquid fertilizer. Repot in spring, usually every 3–4 years.

 In early summer, remove offsets, transfer to individual pots and place in 18–21°C (64–70°F).

Vriesea fenestralis
Distinctive bromeliad, forming a large rosette of shiny, yellowish-green leaves, up to 45cm (18in) long and 5cm (2in) wide, with dark-green veins. The undersides are spotted purplish-red. During summer, it produces a flower spike up to 90cm (3ft) high, bearing tubular, rich sulphur-yellow flowers surrounded by green bracts.

 45–60cm (1½–2ft)

 13–18°C (55–64°F)
Indirect light

 60–75cm (2–2½ft)

 18–27°C (64–80°F)
Indirect light or light shade

 In winter, keep compost just moist and the urn filled with water; in summer, water more freely but ensure compost is well drained, and regularly top up the water in the urn. Feed with weak liquid fertilizer every 4–5 weeks during summer. Repot in spring, usually every 3 years.

 In spring, remove offsets, transfer to individual pots and place in 18–21°C (64–70°F).

Vriesea fosteriana

This has a large rosette of tongue-like, dark bluish-green leaves and develops a stem up to 60cm (2ft) long in summer, bearing pale-yellow flowers with reddish-brown tips.

 45cm (1½ft)

 13–18°C (55–64°F)
Indirect light

 60–75cm (2–2½ft)

 18–27°C (64–80°F)
Indirect light or light shade

 In winter, keep compost just moist and the urn filled with water; in summer, water more freely but ensure compost is well drained, and regularly top up the water in the urn. Feed every 4–5 weeks with weak liquid fertilizer during summer. Repot in spring, usually every 3 years.

 In spring, remove offsets, transfer to individual pots and place in 18–21°C (64–70°F).

Vriesea hieroglyphica

King of the Bromeliads

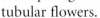

Distinctive bromeliad, with yellowish-green leaves, 60cm (2ft) long and up to 10cm (4in) wide, covered with irregular dark-purple markings. The flowering stem, often 60cm (2ft) long, arises from the plant's centre and bears pale-green bracts and yellow, tubular flowers.

 50–60cm (20–24in)

 13–18°C (55–64°F)
Indirect light

 75–90cm (2½–3ft)

 18–27°C (64–80°F)
Indirect light or light shade

 In winter, keep compost just moist and the urn filled with water; in summer, water more freely but ensure compost is well drained, and regularly top up the water in the urn. Feed every 4–5 weeks with weak liquid fertilizer during summer. Repot in spring, usually every 3 years.

 In spring, remove offsets, transfer to individual pots and place in 18–21°C (64–70°F).

Vriesea splendens
Flaming Sword

This bromeliad has a rosette of sword-shaped, smooth-edged, dark-green leaves with purple-black cross-banding. In late summer, it develops a sword-like head of bright red bracts and yellow flowers.

 38–45cm (15–18in)

 13–18°C (55–64°F)
Indirect light

 30–38cm (12–15in)

 18–27°C (64–80°F)
Indirect light or light shade

 In winter, keep compost just moist and the urn filled with water; in summer, water more freely but ensure the compost is well drained, and regularly top up the water in the urn. Feed every 4–5 weeks with weak liquid fertilizer during summer. Repot in spring, usually every 3 years.

 In spring, remove offsets, transfer to individual pots and place in 18–21°C (64–70°F).

OTHER BROMELIADS AND AIR-PLANTS

Aechmea blumenavii (Urn Plant): 10–15 stiff and strap-like, slightly arching green leaves, 36mm (1½ in) wide, with scaly-white overtones and dark violet at their tops. They form a long tube. Yellow flowers in loose clusters at the tops of long, stiff stems during mid- and late summer.

Billbergia* x *windii: hybrid of *Billbergia nutans*, but smaller and less hardy, and with wider, rigid, grey-green leaves covered in grey scales (as if dusted with flour). Pendent, tubular flowers combine pink and bluish-green, with long, pale-yellow stamens.

Dyckia brevifolia (Pineapple Dyckia): shiny green, stiff, spreading, spine-edged, tapering leaves up to 20cm (8in) long; undersides have silver lines. In late summer, flower stems arise from the plant's sides (not centre) bearing bright orange flowers.

Guzmania sanguinea: urn-forming bromeliad, with broad, flattish rosette of red-tinged leaves and pale-yellow or white central area.

Guzmania sanguinea

INDOOR FERNS

Ferns introduce permanency to displays of plants indoors. They have a long life and retain their foliage throughout the year, so they can be used as focal points – perhaps displayed on special plant stands or in hanging-baskets – as well as creating background colour for other plants. They are not difficult to grow and are ideal in conservatories, where they create a restful ambience.

 HEIGHT SPREAD WINTER SUMMER CARE  PROPAGATION

Adiantum capillus-veneris
Dudder Grass, Maidenhair Fern, Southern Maidenhair Fern, Venus's Hair, Venus-hair Fern
Perennial fern with dainty, delicate, light-green fronds on wiry black stalks.

↕ 15–25cm (6–10in)	❄ 7–13°C (45–55°F) Indirect light
↔ 15–25cm (6–10in)	☼ 13–18°C (55–64°F) Light shade

 In winter, keep compost slightly moist; in summer, water freely and feed every 2–3 weeks with weak liquid fertilizer. Repot in spring when roots fill the pot, usually every 2 years.

 Divide congested plants in spring and place in 13–15°C (55–59°F).

Adiantum raddianum
Delta Maidenhair Fern

Also known as *Adiantum cuneatum*, it is more robust than *Adiantum capillus-veneris*, with long black stalks and pale-green, finely divided, triangular fronds. There are several forms, including 'Fritz Lüthi' (long, narrow fronds with overlapping, curly-edged, slightly blue leaflets) and 'Fragrantissimum' (fragrant fronds).

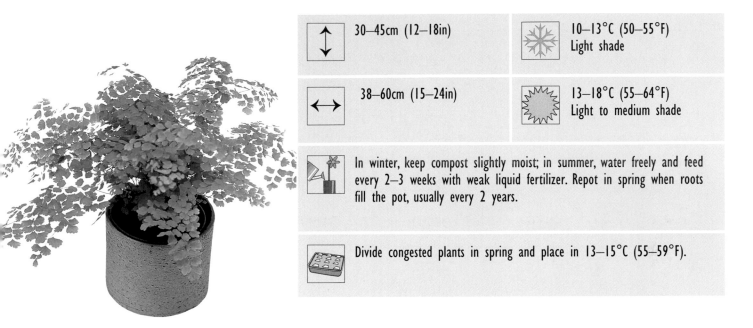

↕ 30–45cm (12–18in)	❄ 10–13°C (50–55°F) Light shade
↔ 38–60cm (15–24in)	☀ 13–18°C (55–64°F) Light to medium shade

In winter, keep compost slightly moist; in summer, water freely and feed every 2–3 weeks with weak liquid fertilizer. Repot in spring when roots fill the pot, usually every 2 years.

Divide congested plants in spring and place in 13–15°C (55–59°F).

Asplenium bulbiferum
Hen-and-chicken Fern, King and Queen Fern, Mother Fern, Mother Spleenwort, Parsley Fern

Distinctive fern with arching stems that bear mid-green, carrot-like fronds with small bulbils along their edges; they tend to weigh down the fronds.

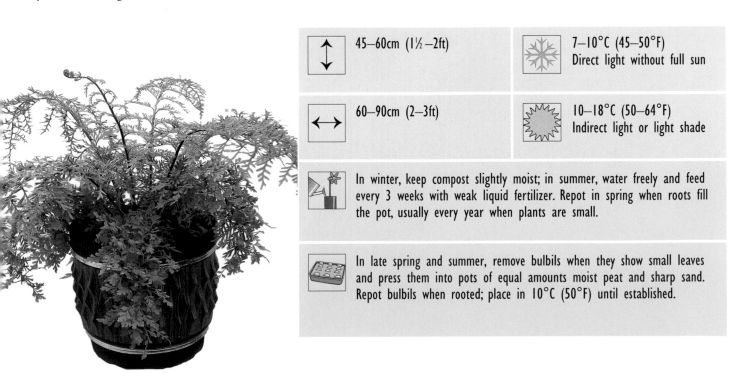

↕ 45–60cm (1½–2ft)	❄ 7–10°C (45–50°F) Direct light without full sun
↔ 60–90cm (2–3ft)	☀ 10–18°C (50–64°F) Indirect light or light shade

In winter, keep compost slightly moist; in summer, water freely and feed every 3 weeks with weak liquid fertilizer. Repot in spring when roots fill the pot, usually every year when plants are small.

In late spring and summer, remove bulbils when they show small leaves and press them into pots of equal amounts moist peat and sharp sand. Repot bulbils when rooted; place in 10°C (50°F) until established.

Asplenium nidus
Bird's Nest Fern, Nest Fern
Large, spoon-shaped, glossy, light- to mid-green leaves form a shuttlecock-like centre.

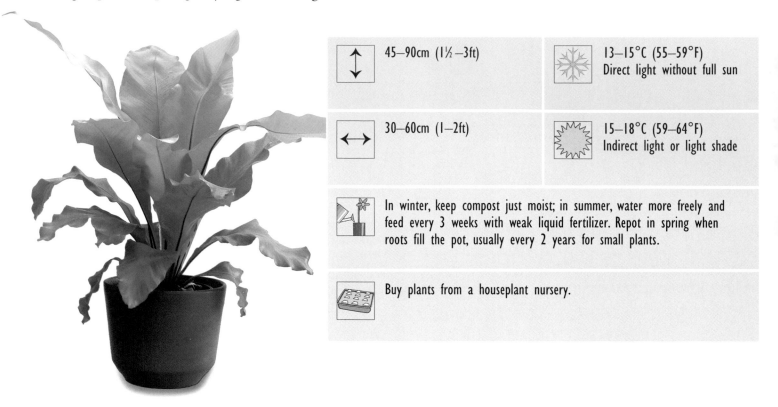

↕	45–90cm (1½–3ft)	❄	13–15°C (55–59°F) Direct light without full sun
↔	30–60cm (1–2ft)	☀	15–18°C (59–64°F) Indirect light or light shade

In winter, keep compost just moist; in summer, water more freely and feed every 3 weeks with weak liquid fertilizer. Repot in spring when roots fill the pot, usually every 2 years for small plants.

Buy plants from a houseplant nursery.

Blechnum gibbum
Hard Fern, Miniature Tree Fern, Rib Fern
Deeply cut, mid-green, stiff, crowded fronds form a spiral at the top in mature plants. Eventually, this fern forms a trunk. *Blechnum brasiliense* is another tree-like fern with large fronds and, eventually, a trunk 90cm (3ft) high.

↕	45–75cm (1½–2½ft)	❄	15–18°C (59–64°F) Full sun, or direct light without full sun
↔	45–75cm (1½–2½ft)	☀	18–24°C (64–75°F) Indirect light or light shade

In winter, keep compost moist but not continually saturated; in summer, water freely but ensure good drainage, and feed every 3–4 weeks with weak liquid fertilizer. Repot in spring when roots fill the pot, usually every 3–4 years.

Buy a young plant from a houseplant nursery.

Cyrtomium falcatum
Holly Fern, Japanese Holly Fern

Arching fronds with stiff, holly-like, dark-green, glossy leaflets, each about 7.5cm (3in) long. The form 'Rochfordianum' has slightly larger, wavy leaflets with serrated edges.

 20–38cm
(8–15in)

 10–13°C (50–55°F)
Direct light without full sun

 38–60cm
(15–24in)

 13–18°C (55–64°F); avoid high
temperatures
Indirect light or light shade

 In winter, keep compost slightly moist, otherwise water freely, especially in spring and early summer when growth resumes. Feed every 3 weeks during summer with weak liquid fertilizer. Repot in spring when roots fill the pot, usually every 2–3 years.

 Divide congested plants in spring and place in 13–15°C (55–59°F).

Davallia canariensis
Deer's-foot Fern, Hare's-foot Fern, Squirrel's-foot Fern

It gains its common names from its fleshy roots covered with pale brown scales. Mid-green, leathery, somewhat triangular fronds eventually hang down.

 30–45cm
(12–18in)

 10–15°C (50–59°F)
Direct light without full sun

 30–38cm (12–15in)

 13–21°C (55–70°F)
Direct light without full sun,
or indirect light

 In winter, keep compost moist but not waterlogged; in summer, water freely but ensure good drainage, and feed every 4 weeks with weak liquid fertilizer. Repot in spring when roots fill the pot, usually every 2–3 years.

 Divide congested plants in spring and place in 13–15°C (55–59°F).

Nephrolepis exaltata
Sword Fern

Ideal and resilient fern for indoors, with long, tapering, usually erect fronds and several attractive forms (*see* box).

 45–75cm (1½ –2½ft)

 10–13°C (50–55°F)
Direct light without full sun

 45–90cm (1½ –3ft)

 13–18°C (55–64°F)
Direct light without full sun, or indirect light

 In winter, keep compost slightly moist; in summer, water freely and feed every 2–3 weeks with weak liquid fertilizer. Repot in spring when roots fill the pot, usually every 2–3 years. When already in a large pot, tease away some of the compost and repot into a same-sized pot, adding some fresh compost.

 Divide congested plants in spring and place in 13–15°C (55–59°F).

Attractive forms of Nephrolepis exaltata (Sword Fern)

Nephrolepis exaltata **'Bostoniensis'** (Boston Fern): graceful fern, with arching fronds (wider than the species).

Nephrolepis exaltata **'Marshallii'** : broad, densely crested, pale-green fronds.

Nephrolepis exaltata **'Rooseveltii'**: distinctive and attractive, with large wavy-edged leaflets.

Nephrolepis exaltata **'Whitmanii'** (Lace Fern): frilled, deeply cut fronds with a feather-like nature.

Right: Nephrolepis exaltata 'Rooseveltii'

Pellaea rotundifolia
Button Fern, New Zealand Cliff Brake
Unusual fern with small, shiny, button-like, slightly waxy, dark-green leaves along wiry stems.

↕ 25–30cm (10–12in)	❄ 10–13°C (50–55°F) Direct light without full sun
↔ 30–38cm (12–15in)	☀ 13–18°C (55–64°F) Direct light without full sun, or indirect light

In winter, keep compost slightly moist; in summer, water freely but avoid waterlogging, and feed every 3 weeks with weak liquid fertilizer. Repot in spring when roots fill the pot, usually every 2–3 years.

Divide congested plants in spring, but not into very small pieces; place in 13–15°C (55–59°F).

Phyllitis scolopendrium
Deer-tongue Fern, Hart's-tongue Fern
Now known as *Asplenium scolopendrium* and earlier as *Scolopendrium vulgare*, this relatively hardy fern's fronds resemble long, shiny-green tongues. Several forms have intricately shaped fronds, including 'Crispum' (edges crisped and waved) and 'Cristatum' (branched and crested tips). It is mainly the cristated forms that are grown indoors.

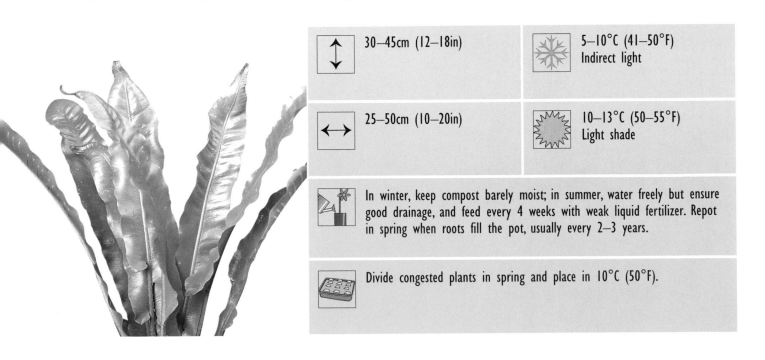

↕ 30–45cm (12–18in)	❄ 5–10°C (41–50°F) Indirect light
↔ 25–50cm (10–20in)	☀ 10–13°C (50–55°F) Light shade

In winter, keep compost barely moist; in summer, water freely but ensure good drainage, and feed every 4 weeks with weak liquid fertilizer. Repot in spring when roots fill the pot, usually every 2–3 years.

Divide congested plants in spring and place in 10°C (50°F).

Platycerium bifurcatum
Stag Horn Fern

Also known as *Platycerium alcicorne*, this distinctive, tender fern develops antler-like, mid-green fronds covered with minute hairs. It is best displayed attached to a piece of wood or cork secured to a wall in a conservatory, or it can be suspended. When young, it can be grown in a pot. *Platycerium grande* (Elk Horn Fern) is similar but larger and may reach 1.5m (5ft) or more wide.

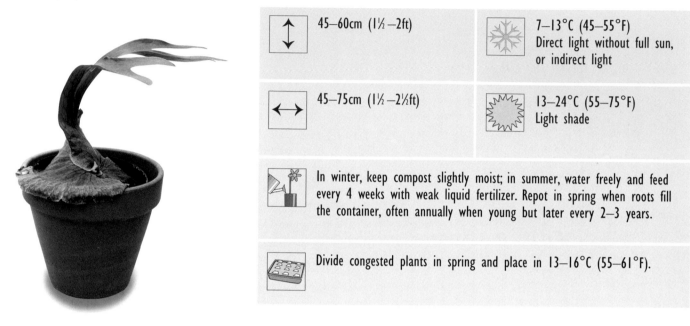

↕ 45–60cm (1½–2ft)	❄ 7–13°C (45–55°F) Direct light without full sun, or indirect light
↔ 45–75cm (1½–2½ft)	☀ 13–24°C (55–75°F) Light shade

In winter, keep compost slightly moist; in summer, water freely and feed every 4 weeks with weak liquid fertilizer. Repot in spring when roots fill the container, often annually when young but later every 2–3 years.

Divide congested plants in spring and place in 13–16°C (55–61°F).

Pteris cretica
Cretan Brake Fern, Ribbon Fern

Strap-shaped leaflets form light-green fronds. There are several attractive forms, including 'Albolineata' (Variegated Table Fern) with white bands along its midribs. Some have cockscomb-tipped fronds.

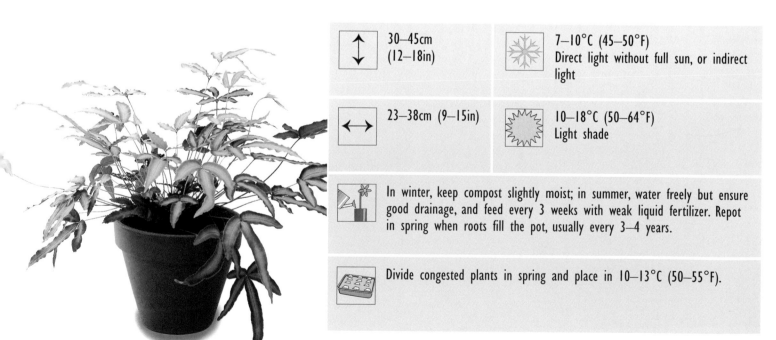

↕ 30–45cm (12–18in)	❄ 7–10°C (45–50°F) Direct light without full sun, or indirect light
↔ 23–38cm (9–15in)	☀ 10–18°C (50–64°F) Light shade

In winter, keep compost slightly moist; in summer, water freely but ensure good drainage, and feed every 3 weeks with weak liquid fertilizer. Repot in spring when roots fill the pot, usually every 3–4 years.

Divide congested plants in spring and place in 10–13°C (50–55°F).

Pteris ensiformis
Sword Brake

This has slender, ribbon-like, deep green fronds. It is usually grown in the form 'Victoriae' (Silver Lace Fern, Victoria Brake Fern and Silver-leaf Fern), with fronds that reveal white midribs.

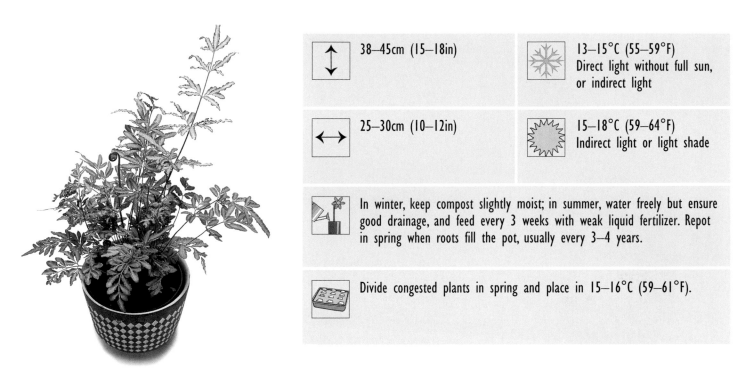

38–45cm (15–18in)

25–30cm (10–12in)

13–15°C (55–59°F)
Direct light without full sun, or indirect light

15–18°C (59–64°F)
Indirect light or light shade

In winter, keep compost slightly moist; in summer, water freely but ensure good drainage, and feed every 3 weeks with weak liquid fertilizer. Repot in spring when roots fill the pot, usually every 3–4 years.

Divide congested plants in spring and place in 15–16°C (59–61°F).

Pteris quadriaurita
Silvery Fern, Silvery Lace Fern, Silver Brake

Usually grown in the form *Pteris quadriaurita argyraea*, also known as *Pteris biaurita argyraea* and frequently sold as *Pteris argyraea*, it has long, grey-green fronds marked with light greenish-white bands along the centre.

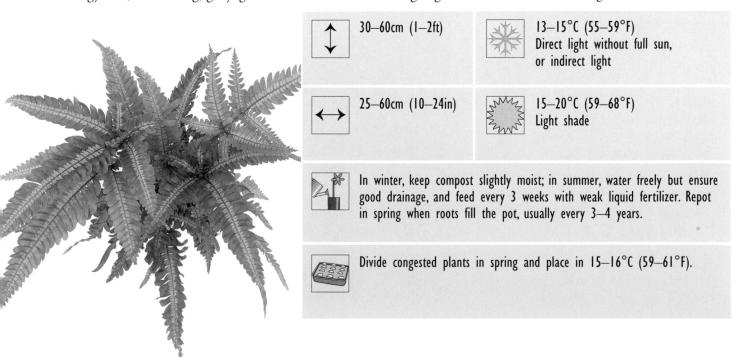

30–60cm (1–2ft)

25–60cm (10–24in)

13–15°C (55–59°F)
Direct light without full sun, or indirect light

15–20°C (59–68°F)
Light shade

In winter, keep compost slightly moist; in summer, water freely but ensure good drainage, and feed every 3 weeks with weak liquid fertilizer. Repot in spring when roots fill the pot, usually every 3–4 years.

Divide congested plants in spring and place in 15–16°C (59–61°F).

Pteris tremula
Australian Bracken, Australian Trembling Fern, Poor Man's Cibotium, Shaking Brake, Tender Brake, Turawera
This plant has slim, arching, triangular, bright-green feathery fronds.

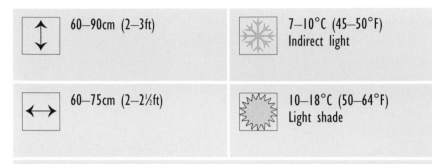

↕ 60–90cm (2–3ft)	❄ 7–10°C (45–50°F) Indirect light
↔ 60–75cm (2–2½ft)	☀ 10–18°C (50–64°F) Light shade

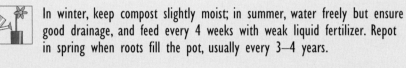
In winter, keep compost slightly moist; in summer, water freely but ensure good drainage, and feed every 4 weeks with weak liquid fertilizer. Repot in spring when roots fill the pot, usually every 3–4 years.

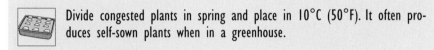
Divide congested plants in spring and place in 10°C (50°F). It often produces self-sown plants when in a greenhouse.

OTHER INDOOR FERNS

Adiantum hispidulum (Australian Maidenhair, Rose Maidenhair): distinctive, with long fronds; coppery-pink when young.

Asplenium flabellifolium (Necklace Fern): pale-green, narrow fronds; ideal for planting in indoor hanging-basket.

Didymochlaena truncatula (Cloak Fern): leathery, brownish-green fronds; it grows well in dense shade.

Phlebodium aureum (Golden Polypody, Rabbit's-foot Fern): eventually large, with a rather sprawling nature and mid-green fronds.

Polystichum auriculatum (Prickly Shield Fern): upright, tapering fronds with pointed ends.

Didymochlaena truncatula

GLOSSARY

Acaricide Chemical used to kill mites, such as red spiders

Acid Soils and composts with pH below 7.0

Aerial roots Roots appearing from a stem above soil/compost level, e.g. Philodendrons, *Monstera deliciosa* (Swiss Cheese Plant), ivies and some orchids

Air layering Method of propagating single-stemmed houseplants, such as *Ficus elastica* (Rubber Plant)

Alkaline Soils and composts with pH above 7.0

Annual Plant that completes its life cycle in a single year – seeds germinate, plants grow and produce flowers within one growing season

Anther Part of a stamen, the male reproductive part of a flower

Aphids Often known as greenfly, they cluster on stems, shoots, leaves and flowers, sucking sap and causing damage

Areole Unique to cacti, they are modified side-shoots in the form of small, cushion-like, usually raised areas; spines or hairs develop from them

Asexual Non-sexual, sometimes used to refer to vegetative propagation, e.g. cuttings and division

Axil Junction between leaf and stem, from where flower stems and side-shoots may develop

Biennial Plant that makes its initial growth during one year and only flowers during the following year

Bleeding Loss of sap from some plants after they are cut

Bloom Two meanings: either a flower or a powdery covering

Bonsai Art of growing dwarfed shrubs and trees in small containers

Bottle gardening Growing plants indoors in enclosed environments created by large glass jars, e.g. carboys

Bottom heat Warming of rooting mixture from below to encourage rapid root development

Botrytis Fungal disease also known as grey mould

Bract Modified leaf associated with flowers; some act as protection for a flower, others take the place of petals to become the main attraction, e.g. *Euphorbia pulcherrima* (Poinsettia)

Bud Tightly packed, immature shoot or flower

Bulb Food storage organ with a bud-like structure formed of fleshy scales attached at their bases to a basal plate, e.g. tulip

Bulbil Immature miniature bulb, usually at the base of a bulb; some plants – e.g. *Asplenium bulbiferum* (Mother Fern) – have small plantlets on their leaves that are known as bulbils

Cactus (plural: cacti) Succulent plants belonging to *Cactaceae* family; characterized by having areoles

Calcicole Plant that likes lime

Calcifuge Plant that dislikes lime

Calyx Protective outer ring of flower parts, usually green

Capillary action Passage of water upward through soil/potting compost: the finer the soil particles, the higher the rise of moisture (the same principle is used in self-watering systems)

Carboy Large, round or pear-shaped glass bottle used as a container for plants

Cladode Modified, flattened stem that takes the form and function of a leaf

Compost Two meanings: the medium in which plants grow when in pots (known as potting soil in North America); material produced after decomposition of vegetable waste, which is then dug into the soil or used as a mulch

Corm Swollen stem bases often classified with bulbs, but structurally different, e.g. crocuses, freesias

Crock Piece of broken clay pot put in the base of a clay pot to prevent the drainage hole from becoming blocked

Cultivar Plant produced in cultivation and indicating a 'cultivated variety'. Earlier, all variations, whether produced naturally in the wild or within cultivation, were known as 'varieties'

Cutting Vegetative method of increasing plants, by which a severed piece of a parent plant is encouraged to develop roots

Damping off Disease that usually attacks seedlings soon after germination

Dead heading Removal of dead or faded flowers to keep a plant tidy and encourage further flower development

Dibber Rounded gardening tool for making holes; used for pricking out seedlings and inserting cuttings in seed-trays and pots

Division Vegetative method of propagation involving root division

Epiphyte Plant that grows on another but is not parasitic, e.g. some orchids and bromeliads

Fern Perennial, flowerless plant that produces spores

Foliar feed Fertilizer applied to foliage

Fronds Leaves of a fern or palm

Fungicide Chemical used to combat fungal diseases

Genus Group of plants with similar botanical characteristics; within a genus are one or more species, each with slightly different characteristics

Germination Process that occurs within a seed when given adequate moisture, air and warmth; the seed-coat ruptures and a seed-leaf grows upward toward the light while a root develops and grows downward (to most gardeners, germination is when they see seed-leaves appearing through the surface of compost/soil)

Glochid Small, hooked hair that grows on some cacti

Heel Pieces of older wood attached to the base of some half-ripe (semi-mature, semi-hardwood) cuttings, which need to be trimmed to remove whisker-like growths

Humidity Amount of moisture in the atmosphere – the higher the temperature, the more moisture air retains

Insecticide Chemical that kills insects

Loam Mixture of sand, clay, silt and decomposed organic material

Mist-spraying Using a sprayer to create a fine mist of clean water around plants to increase humidity

Neutral Neither acid nor alkaline

Node Leaf joint or position where a shoot grows from a stem or main branch

Offset Young plant that arises naturally around its parent, e.g. some bromeliads, bulbs and Houseleeks (*sempervivums*)

Peat Partly decomposed vegetable material, usually acid, often used in potting and seed composts

Pesticide Chemical compound for killing insects and other pests

Petiole Leaf-stalk

pH Logarithmic scale used to define the acidity or alkalinity of soil. Chemically, neutral is 7.0, with figures above indicating increasing alkalinity, and below increasing acidity. Most plants grow well at 6.5

Plantlet An offset produced on a plant's leaves or stems

Pot bound When a plant fills its container with roots and has no further room in which they can grow; it is usually repotted at this stage

Potting-on Transfer of an established plant from one pot to another

Potting soil American term for potting compost

Potting-up Transfer of a young plant from a seed-tray into a pot

Pricking-out Transfer of seedlings from a seed-tray into another seed-tray or pot to give them more space

Propagation Raising of new plants

Repotting Moving a plant that fills its existing pot with roots into a larger one

Rhizome Horizontal stems, underground or partly above; may be slender (Lily-of-the Valley) or thick and corrugated (Bearded Irises)

Root ball The potting compost in which a houseplant grows, together with its roots

Seed leaf First leaf (sometimes two) appearing after germination

Seedling Young plant with a single, unbranched stem, produced after a seed germinates

Sharp sand Sometimes known as concreting sand, it has particles with a sharp nature to ensure good drainage and aeration

Species Group of plants that breed together and have the same characteristics. Species belong to a genus, which can be formed of one or more species. Within a species, there may be several cultivars

Stigma Female part of a flower that receives pollen from the male part

Succulent Any plant with thick, fleshy leaves

Top-dressing Removal of compost from the surface of plants in large containers and replacing it with fresh compost. Plants are usually top-dressed because they are too large to be repotted into fresh compost and a larger pot

Urn Leaves at the centre of bromeliads that form 'vases' through which plants can be watered and fed

Variety *see* Cultivar

Vegetative propagation Method of increasing plants, including division of roots, layering and taking cuttings

INDEX

PHOTOGRAPHIC CREDITS